ETHNIC COOKBOOK

EXPERIENCE THE WORLD'S BEST CULINARY CONTRIBUTIONS AT HOME WITH EASY ETHNIC RECIPES FROM EVERY REGION OF THE WORLD

By
BookSumo Press
Copyright © by Saxonberg Associates

Published by
BookSumo Press, a DBA of Saxonberg Associates
http://www.booksumo.com/

ABOUT THE AUTHOR.

BookSumo Press is a publisher of unique, easy, and healthy cookbooks.

Our cookbooks span all topics and all subjects. If you want a deep dive into the possibilities of cooking with any type of ingredient. Then BookSumo Press is your go to place for robust yet simple and delicious cookbooks and recipes. Whether you are looking for great tasting pressure cooker recipes or authentic ethic and cultural food. BookSumo Press has a delicious and easy cookbook for you.

With simple ingredients, and even simpler step-by-step instructions BookSumo cookbooks get everyone in the kitchen chefing delicious meals.

BookSumo is an independent publisher of books operating in the beautiful Garden State (NJ) and our team of chefs and kitchen experts are here to teach, eat, and be merry!

INTRODUCTION

Welcome to *The Effortless Chef Series*! Thank you for taking the time to purchase this cookbook.

Come take a journey into the delights of easy cooking. The point of this cookbook and all BookSumo Press cookbooks is to exemplify the effortless nature of cooking simply.

In this book we focus on ethnic cooking. You will find that even though the recipes are simple, the taste of the dishes are quite amazing.

So will you take an adventure in simple cooking? If the answer is yes please consult the table of contents to find the dishes you are most interested in.

Once you are ready, jump right in and start cooking.

— BookSumo Press

TABLE OF CONTENTS

Any Issues? Contact Us

If you find that something important to you is missing from this book please contact us at info@booksumo.com.

We will take your concerns into consideration when the 2nd edition of this book is published. And we will keep you updated!

— BookSumo Press

LEGAL NOTES

COMMON ABBREVIATIONS

cup(s)	C.
tablespoon	tbsp
teaspoon	tsp
ounce	oz.
pound	lb

*All units used are standard American measurements

CHAPTER 1: EASY ETHNIC RECIPES

ASH-E-JOW

(BARLEY SOUP)

Ingredients:2 quarts chicken stock

- 2 tbsps vegetable oil
- one medium onion, diced
- one cup uncooked pearl barley
- one tsp turmeric
- one lime, juiced
- 1/4 cup tomato paste
- salt, according to your preference
- ground black pepper, according to your preference
- one cup diced carrots
- 1/2 cup sour cream
- 1/2 cup chopped fresh parsley
- 8 lime wedges

Directions:
- Get a pot that can be covered. Heat chicken stock until simmering.
- Get another pot, heat veggie oil. Fry onions until translucent.

- Combine pearl barley and stir for 1 min.
- Combine the following ingredients: pepper, heated chicken stock, salt, turmeric, tomato paste, and juiced lime.
- Heat until boiling. Turn heat to low. Simmer for 1 hr.
- Combine carrots, cook for thirty mins.
- Get a bowl and add some sour cream to it.
- Take 1/2 a cup of soup, and combine it with the sour cream.
- Combine both pots into one. Add fresh parsley.
- Serve with lime.

NOTE: If you notice that your soup gets too hard or thick, then to fix this, you only have to mix in some extra water.

Serving Size: 8 servings

Preparation	Cooking	Total Time
10 mins	2 hrs	2 hrs 10 mins

Nutritional Information:

Calories	193 kcal
Carbohydrates	28.3 g
Cholesterol	9 mg
Fat	.2 g
Fiber	4.3 g
Protein	5.5 g
Sodium	178 mg

* Percent Daily Values are based on a 2,000 calorie diet.

KHORESH FESENJAN

(CHICKEN POMEGRANATE STEW)

Ingredients:
- 2 tbsps olive oil
- one 1/2 lbs chicken legs, cut up
- one white onion, thinly sliced
- 1/2 lb walnuts, toasted and finely ground in a food processor
- one tsp salt
- 4 cups pomegranate juice
- 1/2 tsp cardamom (optional)
- 2 tbsps sugar (optional)

Directions:
- Get a skillet heat olive oil.
- For 20 mins fry onions, and chicken.
- Add: cardamom, walnut puree, pomegranate juice, and salt.
- Heat until boiling. Set heat to low and cover skillet. Let everything simmer for 1.5 hrs.
- Add some sugar.
- Simmer for 30 more mins.
- Serve and enjoy.

NOTE: If the contents become too thick then make sure you add some additional warm water.

Serving Size: 6 servings

Preparation	Cooking	Total Time
15 mins	2 hrs 30 mins	2 hrs 45 mins

Nutritional Information:

Calories	785 kcal
Carbohydrates	95.4 g
Cholesterol	64 mg
Fat	39 g
Fiber	2.9 g
Protein	24.4 g
Sodium	445 mg

* Percent Daily Values are based on a 2,000 calorie diet.

Maast-o Khiar

(Cucumber Yogurt)

Ingredients:
- one (32 oz) container plain yogurt
- 3 cucumbers, peels removed and diced
- one clove garlic, minced
- one shallot, finely chopped
- 5 tbsps dried dill weed
- one tsp salt
- one tsp pepper

Directions:
- Get a bowl, mix the following: shallot, yogurt, garlic, and cucumbers.
- Add: pepper, dill, and salt.
- Refrigerate for one hour.
- Plate and enjoy.

Serving Size: 16 servings

Preparation	Cooking	Total Time
15 mins	1 hr	1 hr 15 mins

Nutritional Information:

Calories	46 kcal
Carbohydrates	6.3 g
Cholesterol	3 mg
Fat	0.9 g
Fiber	0.7 g
Protein	3.8 g
Sodium	188 mg

* Percent Daily Values are based on a 2,000 calorie diet.

KEBABS PERSIAN STYLE

Ingredients:
- one (8 oz) container plain low-fat yogurt
- one onion, chopped
- 1/2 tsp dried mint
- 2 lbs beef top sirloin, cut into large cubes

Directions:
- Get a bowl, combine the following: mint, yogurt, and onion.
- Add beef cubes.
- Cover and refrigerate for 6 hrs.
- Heat a grill or grilling plate.
- Place beef pieces on skewers and grill them for 15 mins.
- Plate and enjoy.

NOTE: If using a grilling plate increase the cooking time of the beef slightly.

Serving Size: 6 servings

Preparation	Cooking	Total Time
15 mins	15 mins	6 hrs 30 mins

Nutritional Information:

Calories	263 kcal
Carbohydrates	4.4 g
Cholesterol	83 mg
Fat	14.4 g
Fiber	0.3 g
Protein	27.1 g
Sodium	84 mg

* Percent Daily Values are based on a 2,000 calorie diet.

PERSIAN MELON SALAD

Ingredients:
- one honeydew melon, fruit removed with a melon baller
- one cantaloupe, fruit removed with a melon baller
- 1/4 watermelon, fruit removed with a melon baller
- one bunch grapes
- one pineapple - peeled, cored, and cut into chunks
- 2 tbsps pickled ginger
- one cup fresh orange juice
- 1/4 cup fresh lime juice
- one tbsp white sugar
- 1/4 cup chopped fresh mint
- one pint fresh strawberries, hulled (optional)
- 4 sprigs fresh mint for garnish

Directions:
- Get a bowl mix the following: chopped mint, honeydew, sugar, watermelon, lime juice, grapes, orange juice, pineapple, and pickled ginger.
- Cover the bowl refrigerate for one hour.
- Add strawberries and mint.
- Enjoy.

Serving Size: 12 servings

Preparation	Cooking	Total Time
30 mins		1 hr 30 mins

Nutritional Information:

Calories	194 kcal
Carbohydrates	48.8 g
Cholesterol	0 mg
Fat	0.9 g
Fiber	4.3 g
Protein	2.8 g
Sodium	47 mg

* Percent Daily Values are based on a 2,000 calorie diet.

KEBABS PERSIAN STYLE II

Ingredients:
- 2 lbs beef tenderloin
- one onion, chopped
- one tbsp salt, pepper
- one juiced lime

Directions:
- Dice beef into cubes.
- Get a bowl, combine the beef pieces with the following ingredients: lime juice, onion, black pepper, and salt.
- Cover and marinate beef for 8 hours.
- Heat a grill or grilling plate. Put eight cubes on each skewer.
- Allow the beef pieces to grill for about 4 mins per side. Total time for each piece should be about 16 mins.
- Plate and enjoy.

NOTE: If using a grilling plate increase the cooking time of the beef according to your preference.

Serving Size: 4 servings

Preparation	Cooking	Total Time
20 mins	15 mins	35 mins

Nutritional Information:

Calories	297 kcal
Carbohydrates	3.4 g
Cholesterol	113 mg
Fat	13.5 g
Fiber	0.6 g
Protein	38.4 g
Sodium	1830 mg

* Percent Daily Values are based on a 2,000 calorie diet.

FESENJUN

Ingredients:
- 2 tbsps olive oil
- one onion, finely chopped
- 4 skinless, boneless chicken breast halves
- one cup finely ground walnuts
- one (10 fluid oz) bottle pomegranate paste or syrup

Directions:
- Get a skillet heat olive oil.
- Fry onions until soft.
- Add chicken to the onions. Fry chicken until brown on all sides. Put aside.
- Add walnuts to the oil and fry for 10 mins.
- Add chicken onions with walnuts and add pomegranate paste.
- Set heat to low. Let contents simmer for 20 mins while covered. Stir occasionally.
- Plate and enjoy.

Serving Size: 4 servings

Preparation	Cooking	Total Time
15 mins	30 mins	45 mins

Nutritional Information:

Calories	572 kcal
Carbohydrates	53.2 g
Cholesterol	61 mg
Fat	28.8 g
Fiber	2.5 g
Protein	27.8 g
Sodium	53 mg

* Percent Daily Values are based on a 2,000 calorie diet.

Sabzi Polo

(Herb Rice with Fava Beans)

Ingredients:
- 6 cups water
- 4 cups uncooked long-grain white rice
- 3 tbsps vegetable oil
- 1/2 cup water
- one bunch fresh dill, chopped
- one bunch fresh parsley, chopped
- one bunch fresh cilantro, chopped
- 2 cups fresh or frozen fava beans
- ground turmeric according to your preference
- ground cinnamon according to your preference
- one tsp salt
- one tsp pepper

Directions:
- Get saucepan. Add water. Heat until boiling.
- Rinse rice under water, until the water runs clear.
- Add rice to boiling water.
- Boil rice until it begins to float. Then drain the water and leave the rice in the pot. Add oil and ½ cup of water.
- Also add the following: pepper, dill, salt, parsley, cinnamon, cilantro, turmeric, and fava beans.
- Fry for 5 mins.

- Set heat to low. Cover the pot. Let everything cook for 45 mins.
- Let everything cool. Plate and enjoy.

NOTE: The bottom part of the rice should be crispy like our other recipe, Lubia Polo, make sure to enjoy this very tasty part.

Serving Size: 16 servings

Preparation	Cooking	Total Time
20 mins	55 mins	1 hr 15 mins

Nutritional Information:

Calories	234 kcal
Carbohydrates	44.7 g
Cholesterol	0 mg
Fat	3.1 g
Fiber	2.1 g
Protein	5.5 g
Sodium	214 mg

* Percent Daily Values are based on a 2,000 calorie diet.

Yogurt Salad Persian Style

Ingredients:
- one (32 oz) container plain yogurt
- 2 tbsps dried dill weed
- 2 cloves garlic, minced
- salt and black pepper according to your preference
- one cucumber (with seeds and peel removed, and chopped)

Directions:
- Get a bowl, combine the following ingredients in it: pepper, yogurt, salt, dill weed, and garlic.
- Add cucumber.
- Place a lid on the bowl and refrigerate for 8 hours.
- Plate and serve.

Serving Size: 8 servings

Preparation	Cooking	Total Time
10 mins		8 hrs 10 mins

Nutritional Information:

Calories	78 kcal
Carbohydrates	9.3 g
Cholesterol	7 mg
Fat	1.8 g
Fiber	0.3 g
Protein	6.3 g
Sodium	154 mg

* Percent Daily Values are based on a 2,000 calorie diet.

HERBED POMEGRANATE SALSA

Ingredients:
- one 1/2 sprigs fresh mint, chopped
- one 1/2 bunches fresh cilantro, chopped
- one 1/2 bunches Italian flat leaf parsley, chopped
- one small red onion, chopped
- one pomegranate, skin and light-colored membrane removed
- 6 tbsps fresh lime juice
- 2 tsps grated lime zest
- one jalapeno pepper, chopped
- one serrano pepper, chopped
- one small tomato, diced
- 2 tbsps olive oil
- salt according to your preference
- ground white pepper according to your preference

Directions:
- Get a bowl combine: olive oil, mint, tomato, cilantro, serrano pepper, Italian parsley, jalapeno pepper, red onion, lime zest, pomegranate, and juiced lime.
- Place a lid over your mixture and put it in the frig for about two hrs.
- Once everything has chilled-out nicely serve and enjoy.

Serving Size: 4 servings

Preparation	Cooking	Total Time
20 mins		2 hrs 20 mins

Nutritional Information:

Calories	119 kcal
Carbohydrates	14 g
Cholesterol	0 mg
Fat	7.3 g
Fiber	2.5 g
Protein	2.1 g
Sodium	123 mg

* Percent Daily Values are based on a 2,000 calorie diet.

YAZDI CAKES

Ingredients:
- 2 cups all-purpose flour
- one tsp baking powder
- 4 eggs
- one 1/4 cups white sugar
- one 1/2 cups butter, melted
- one cup plain yogurt
- one 1/2 tsps ground cardamom
- one tbsp rose water
- 1/2 cup blanched slivered almonds
- one 1/2 tbsps chopped pistachio nuts

Directions:
- Set oven to 375 degrees F.
- Grab a sifter and a bowl. Sift baking powder and flour into this bowl. Set aside.
- Get a baking dish for cupcakes coat with nonstick cooking spray or veggie oil.
- Get a bowl and mix sugar and eggs. Place bowl on top of a pan of simmering water.
- Inside of this bowl mix your eggs with a mixer or whisk for eight mins.
- Remove from heat and continue whisking for 10 mins.
- Add: rose water, butter, cardamom, and yogurt. Now you want to combine the flour and also the almonds.
- Grab a scoop and put the contents into the cupcake sections.

- Fill each cupcake section but leave some space for expansion.
- Add a covering of pistachios. Enter the cakes into the oven for about 30 mins.
- Enjoy after cool.

Serving Size: 24 cakes

Preparation	Cooking	Total Time
20 mins	25 mins	45 mins

Nutritional Information:

Calories	215 kcal
Carbohydrates	19.9 g
Cholesterol	62 mg
Fat	14 g
Fiber	0.6 g
Protein	3.4 g
Sodium	121 mg

* Percent Daily Values are based on a 2,000 calorie diet.

ISKENDER KEBABS

Ingredients
- 4 pita bread rounds
- 1 tbsp olive oil
- 4 skinless, boneless chicken breast halves - chopped
- 2 medium onion, chopped
- 1 clove garlic, minced
- 1 (10.75 ounce) can tomato puree
- ground cumin to taste
- salt to taste
- ground black pepper to taste
- 1/2 cup butter, melted
- 1 cup Greek yogurt
- 1/4 cup chopped fresh parsley

Directions
- Preheat your oven to 350 degrees F and bake pita bread in it for some time before cutting it down into small pieces.
- Cook garlic, chicken and onion in hot oil for some time before adding tomato puree, pepper, salt and cumin, and cooking it for another ten minutes.
- On top of pita bread in a serving platter; put chicken mixture and some butter.
- Garnish with some parsley and yoghurt before you serve it.

Serving: 4

Timing Information:

Preparation	Cooking	Total Time
15 mins	15 mins	30 mins

Nutritional Information:

Calories	667 kcal
Carbohydrates	48.6 g
Cholesterol	144 mg
Fat	36.2 g
Fiber	3.9 g
Protein	37.3 g
Sodium	886 mg

* Percent Daily Values are based on a 2,000 calorie diet.

Homemade Harissa

(Classical North African Style)

Ingredients

- 6 oz. bird's eye chilies, seeded and stems removed
- 12 cloves garlic, peeled
- 1 tbsp coriander, ground
- 1 tbsp ground cumin
- 1 tbsp salt
- 1 tbsp dried mint
- 1/2 C. chopped fresh cilantro
- 1/2 C. olive oil

Directions

- Add the following to the bowl a food processor: chilies, cilantro, garlic, salt mint, coriander, and cumin.
- Pulse the mix until it is smooth then add in some olive oil and pulse the mix a few more times.
- Place the mix in jar and top everything with the rest of the oil.
- Enjoy.

Amount per serving (40 total)

Timing Information:

Preparation	
Cooking	20 m
Total Time	20 m

Nutritional Information:

Calories	28 kcal
Fat	2.8
Carbohydrates	0.9g
Protein	0.2 g
Cholesterol	0 m
Sodium	176 m

* Percent Daily Values are based on a 2,000 calorie diet.

Homemade Harissa
(Classical Tunisian Style)

Ingredients

- 11 oz. dried red chile peppers, stems removed, seeds, removed
- 3/4 C. chopped garlic
- 2 C. caraway seed
- 1/2 tsp ground coriander seed
- 2 tsps salt

Directions

- Let your chilies sit submerged in water for 30 mins then remove the liquids.
- Now add the following to the bowl of a food processor: salt, pepper, coriander, garlic, and caraway.
- Puree the mix then place everything into a Mason jar and top the mix with a bit of oil.
- Place the lid on the jar tightly and put everything in the fridge.
- Enjoy.

Amount per serving (192 total)

Timing Information:

Preparation	
Cooking	40 m
Total Time	1 h

Nutritional Information:

Calories	10 kcal
Fat	0.3 g
Carbohydrates	1.9g
Protein	0.4 g
Cholesterol	0 m
Sodium	26 m

* Percent Daily Values are based on a 2,000 calorie diet.

PLUMS, TOMATOES, AND SAMOSAS (INDIAN)

Ingredients

- 2 tbsps pine nuts
- 2 C. coarsely chopped plums
- 2 tbsps shallots, chopped
- 1 1/2 tsps olive oil
- 1 1/2 tsps butter
- 2 medium tomatoes, quartered
- 1 garlic clove, chopped
- 1 tbsp sugar
- 1/2 tsp harissa
- 1 thyme, sprig
- 1 vanilla bean
- 1/2 tsp chopped fresh basil
- 1/4 tsp salt
- cooking spray
- 1/2 C. thinly sliced yellow onion
- 1 lb Yukon gold potato, peeled and cut into 1/4-inch cubes
- 1/2 C. carrot, chopped
- 2 1/2 tsps red curry paste
- 1 garlic clove, diced

- 1 C. water
- 1/3 C. light coconut milk
- 2 tsps fresh lime juice
- 1/4 tsp salt
- 1 tsp ground turmeric
- 1/2 tsp ground ginger
- 1/2 tsp ground cinnamon
- 6 3/4 oz. all-purpose flour
- 1/2 tsp salt
- 1/4 tsp baking soda
- 1/4 C. hot water
- 6 tbsps fresh lemon juice
- 7 tsps peanut oil, divided

Directions

- Begin by toasting your pine nuts for 3 mins with no oil in a large pot, then add in the garlic, plums, tomatoes, shallots, butter, and olive oil.
- Get the mixing gently boiling, then set the heat to low, and continue to simmer the mix for 35 mins. Stir the mix every 5 mins.
- Now combine in: the vanilla bean, sugar, thyme, and harissa.
- Stir the mix and continue cooking everything for 25 more mins.

- Now shut the heat, place a lid on the pot, and let the contents sit for 40 mins.
- Take out the vanilla and thyme and throw them away. Then add in 1/4 tsp of salt and the basil. Stir the mix.
- Get a frying pan hot with nonstick spray then begin to fry your potatoes and onions for 7 mins, set the heat to low, and stir in the garlic, curry paste, and carrots.
- Continue to cook the carrots for 7 mins while mixing everything.
- Combine in the coconut milk and 1 C. of water and get the mix boiling.
- Once the mix is boiling set the heat to low, and continue to simmer everything for 17 mins until most of the moisture has cooked out.
- Now combine in 1/4 tsp of salt and the lime juice.
- Stir the mix then place everything into a bowl.
- Let the potatoes lose their heat then mash everything together.
- Get a separate frying pan and begin to toast your cinnamon, turmeric and ginger in it for 1 min then remove the spices to the side.
- Now add the following to the bowl of a food processor: baking soda, flour, 1/2 tsp salt, and toasted cinnamon mix.
- Process the mix a bit to evenly combine it then add in the following: 1 tbsp peanut oil, 1/4 C. hot water, and lemon juice.

- Process the mix again until you have a dough.
- Get a bowl and coat it with nonstick spray and place the dough in the bowl.
- Place a damp kitchen towel over the bowl and let it sit for 20 mins.
- Now break your dough into twelve pieces and flatten each into a circle.
- In the middle of each circle add 2 tbsps of the potato mix. Coat the outside of each piece of dough with some water and shape everything into a semi-circle and seal each, with a fork.
- Do this for all your dough and potato mix.
- Now begin to fry half of the samosas in 2 tsp of hot peanut oil for 5 mins.
- Flip each one and continue frying them for 4 more mins.
- Now fry the rest of the samosas in an additional 2 tsp of oil for the same amount of time.
- Top the samosas, with the harissa mix, when serving them.
- Enjoy.

Amount per serving: 1

Timing Information:

Preparation	2 h
Total Time	4 h

Nutritional Information:

Calories	163.5 g
Cholesterol	1.2mg
Sodium	230.6mg
Carbohydrates	27.5g
Protein	3.1

* Percent Daily Values are based on a 2,000 calorie diet.

APRICOTS AND LAMB

(MOROCCAN)

Ingredients

- 2 tbsps extra-virgin olive oil
- 1 tsp cumin seeds
- 1 onion, thinly sliced
- 4 cloves garlic, crushed
- 1 sweet potato, peeled and diced
- 2 (1 lb) lamb shanks
- 1 (14.4 oz.) can chopped canned tomatoes
- 1 1/4 C. chopped dried apricots
- 1 1/2 tsps harissa
- salt and pepper to taste
- 2 tbsps slivered almonds
- 1 C. quick-cooking couscous
- 2 tbsps extra-virgin olive oil

Directions

- Stir fry your cumin seeds in 2 tbsp of olive oil for 60 secs then add in the sweet potatoes, onions, and garlic.
- Set the heat to low and place a lid on the pot.

- Leave the potatoes for 7 mins and try to stir them at least twice as they cook.
- Place your lamb into the pot and brown the meat all over for about 10 mins then combine in the harissa, tomatoes, and apricots.
- Stir the mix then combine in some pepper and salt. Add a bit more water and get everything boiling.
- Once the mix is boiling, place a lid on the pot, set the heat to low, and cook the mix for 60 mins.
- Stir every 10 mins.
- In a separate pan begin to toast your almonds for 7 mins, with no oil, then place them to the side.
- Get a bowl and add in your couscous. Combine the warm water with the couscous and let everything sit for 7 mins.
- Combine the almonds and 2 tbsps of olive oil with the couscous and place everything into a platter.
- Top the couscous with the lamb, its drippings, and the veggie fruit mix in the pan.
- Enjoy.

Amount per serving (2 total)

Timing Information:

Preparation	10
Cooking	1 h 30 m
Total Time	2 h

Nutritional Information:

Calories	1256 kcal
Fat	54.5 g
Carbohydrates	121.4 mg
Protein	70 g
Cholesterol	179 m
Sodium	824 m

* Percent Daily Values are based on a 2,000 calorie diet.

Spinach Potatoes and Eggs (Tunisian)

Ingredients

- 1/3 C. vegetable oil
- 2 potatoes, peeled and cubed
- 8 oz. diced chicken breast meat
- 1 large onion, diced
- 1 tbsp harissa
- 1 1/2 tsps ras el hanout
- 1/2 C. water
- 1 1/2 tbsps tomato sauce
- 1 tbsp butter
- 1 bunch fresh spinach, washed and chopped
- 8 eggs
- 1 C. frozen peas
- 1/3 C. Parmesan cheese
- 1 pinch salt and pepper to taste

Directions

- Coat a casserole dish with nonstick spray then set your oven to 400 degrees before doing anything else.

- Fry your potatoes in veggie oil for 10 mins then place them to the side.
- Add in the rest of the oil and begin to fry your chicken in it for 3 mins then combine in the onions.
- Keep cooking everything for 7 mins then combine in the butter, harissa, tomato sauce, ras el hanout, and water.
- Stir the mix until it is all evenly combined, then get everything boiling.
- Once the mix is boiling, set the heat to low and place the spinach in.
- Once the spinach is soft shut the heat and place a lid on the pot.
- Get a bowl and whisk your eggs in it then combine in the potatoes, parmesan, and peas.
- Combine this mix with the chicken mix and top everything with some pepper and salt and place the mix into the casserole dish.
- Cook everything in the oven for 25 mins.
- Enjoy.

Amount per serving (12 total)

Timing Information:

Preparation	30 m
Cooking	35 m
Total Time	1 h 30 m

Nutritional Information:

Calories	193 kcal
Fat	11.7
Carbohydrates	11.4
Protein	11.4
Cholesterol	139 m
Sodium	157 m

* Percent Daily Values are based on a 2,000 calorie diet.

Sun Dried Tomatoes, Cinnamon, and Beef Puff Pastry

Ingredients

- 1 onion, cut into 6 pieces
- 1 onion, diced
- 3 lbs beef stewing beef, cut into 3 cm cubes
- 2 tbsps harissa
- 2 tbsps plain flour
- 140 g tomato paste
- 1 C. dry red wine
- 2 C. beef stock
- 2 bay leaves
- 1 cinnamon stick
- 1 C. pitted kalamata olive
- 1/2 C. sun-dried tomato
- 1/4 C. of fresh mint
- 6 sheets frozen butter puff pastry, thawed before using
- 1/4 C. lightly packed brown sugar
- 1 egg, beaten

Directions

- Set your oven to 325 degrees before doing anything else.
- Get a bowl, combine: the harissa and beef.
- Evenly coat the pieces of beef.
- Now brown the beef all over, in oil, in a skillet, then add in the onion and continue frying everything for 5 mins.

- Combine in the tomato paste and cook the mix for 60 more secs.
- Stir in the flour and the beef evenly, and let the contents cook for 60 secs then combine in the cinnamon, bay leaves, stock, and wine.
- Get everything boiling, place a lid on the pot, and put the mix in the oven for 2 hrs.
- Combine in the mint, sun dried tomatoes, and olives.
- Take the dish out of the oven and let everything lose its heat.
- Now set your oven to 400 degrees.
- Coat your 6 pieces of onion with oil and sugar.
- Sear the onions for 60 secs in a skillet then lay out 6 pie dishes.
- Place some beef in each dish and lay your puff pastry over each dish.
- Fold the edges in and place a piece of onion in the middle of each.
- Coat the pies with the eggs and cook them for 30 mins in the oven at 400 degrees.
- Enjoy.

Amount per serving: 6

Timing Information:

Preparation	30 mins
Total Time	32 mins

Nutritional Information:

Calories	2151.4
Cholesterol	202.4mg
Sodium	1504.5mg
Carbohydrates	136.2g
Protein	68.0

* Percent Daily Values are based on a 2,000 calorie diet.

CHIPOTLE CHICKEN BREAST

Ingredients

- 2 tbsps smoked paprika
- 2 cloves garlic, diced
- 1 tsp ground cumin
- 1 tsp caraway seeds
- 1 chipotle pepper in adobo sauce
- 1 tsp harissa
- 4 skinless, boneless chicken breast halves
- 1 tbsp extra-virgin olive oil
- salt and black pepper to taste

Directions

- Get a mortar and pestle and mash the following: adobo sauce, paprika, chipotle pepper, garlic, caraway seeds, and cumin.
- Coat your chicken with this mix, once it is smooth, then place everything in a bowl.
- Place a covering of plastic on the bowl and put everything in the fridge for 5 hrs.

- Get a grill hot and coat the grate with oil, grill your chicken for 6 mins each side, after coating the meat with olive oil, some pepper and salt.
- Enjoy.

Amount per serving (4 total)

Timing Information:

Preparation	20 m
Cooking	10 m
Total Time	4 h 30 m

Nutritional Information:

Calories	178 kcal
Fat	5.6
Carbohydrates	3.2
Protein	28
Cholesterol	68 m
Sodium	101 m

* Percent Daily Values are based on a 2,000 calorie diet.

Paprika Harissa Lemon Fish

Ingredients

- 1 tsp vegetable oil
- 1 lb salmon fillet
- salt and pepper to taste
- 4 thin slices lemon
- 2 thin slices sweet onion, separated into rings
- 1/3 C. mayonnaise
- 1 tsp lemon juice
- 1 tsp harissa
- 1/4 tsp smoked paprika
- 1 tbsp orange juice
- 1 tbsp white wine

Directions

- Grease a casserole dish with oil then set your oven to 425 degrees before doing anything else.
- Coat your salmon with pepper and salt then lay the pieces of fish into the dish. Top the fish with the onion and lemon.
- Get a bowl, combine: paprika, mayo, harissa, and lemon juice.

- Combine the mix until it is smooth then coat your fish with it.
- Add the wine and orange around the fish and cook everything in the oven for 14 mins.
- Now place the fish in a broiler pan and broil everything for 4 mins.
- Enjoy.

Amount per serving (4 total)

Timing Information:

Preparation	20 m
Cooking	15 m
Total Time	35 m

Nutritional Information:

Calories	315 kcal
Fat	22.9 g
Carbohydrates	3.2 mg
Protein	22.9 g
Cholesterol	70 mg
Sodium	262 mg

* Percent Daily Values are based on a 2,000 calorie diet.

PERSIAN COUSCOUS WITH HARISSA AND CURRANTS

Ingredients

- 2 tbsps warm water
- 5 saffron threads, or more to taste
- 1 C. couscous
- 1 C. vegetable broth
- 1 celery stalk, diced
- 1/4 C. dried currants
- 2 tbsps extra-virgin olive oil
- 1 tbsp lemon juice
- 1 tsp harissa, or to taste
- 1/2 tsp ground cumin
- sea salt to taste

Directions

- Let your saffron sit submerged in the warm water.
- Get your couscous boiling in the veggie broth.
- Once the mix is boiling place a lid on the pot, shut the heat, and let everything stand for 10 mins.

- Get a bowl, combine: couscous, saffron mix, sea salt, celery, cumin, currants, harissa, olive oil, and lemon juice.
- Place the mix in the fridge for 1 hr.
- Enjoy.

Amount per serving (4 total)

Timing Information:

Preparation	
Cooking	15 m
Total Time	50 m

Nutritional Information:

Calories	265 kcal
Fat	7.3 g
Carbohydrates	43.2 mg
Protein	6.3 g
Cholesterol	0 mg
Sodium	228 mg

* Percent Daily Values are based on a 2,000 calorie diet.

KALE AND SWEET POTATO STEW

Ingredients

- 1 large onion, diced
- 2 tbsps olive oil
- 8 oz. Spanish chorizo, cut into 1/2 inch pieces
- 3 stalks celery, diced
- 3 carrots, diced
- 2 tsps ground cumin
- 1 tbsp paprika
- 1/2 tsp ground turmeric
- 2 tsps kosher salt
- 1 tsp freshly ground black pepper
- 1 pinch saffron threads
- 5 garlic cloves, diced
- 2 sweet potatoes, peeled and cut into 1-inch pieces
- 8 C. chicken broth
- 4 C. lacinato kale, washed, stemmed, and torn into pieces
- 1 lemon, juiced
- salt and pepper to taste
- 1 pinch harissa, or to taste
- 1 tbsp chopped fresh flat-leaf parsley

Directions

- Stir fry your onions in olive oil, in a large pot, for 10 mins then combine in the chorizo and fry the sausage for 5 more mins.
- Stir in the carrots and celery.

- Continue frying the veggies for 5 mins then combine in: the garlic, cumin, saffron, turmeric, kosher salt, paprika, and black pepper.
- Combine in the spices then continue frying everything for 4 more mins then combine in the broth and sweet potatoes.
- Stir the mix again and get everything boiling.
- Once the mix is boiling, set the heat to low, and simmer the mix for 25 mins.
- Combine in the kale and cook the stew for 12 more mins then add some more pepper, salt, and the lemon juice.
- When serving the stew top it with some parsley and harissa.
- Enjoy.

Amount per serving (8 total)

Timing Information:

Preparation	40 m
Cooking	45 m
Total Time	1 h 25 m

Nutritional Information:

Calories	249 kcal
Fat	15.4 mg
Carbohydrates	18.8 g
Protein	10.4 g
Cholesterol	30 mg
Sodium	1866 mg

* Percent Daily Values are based on a 2,000 calorie diet.

SPICY CARROT PASTE

Ingredients

- 4 large carrots, peeled and roughly chopped
- 2 garlic cloves, peeled and chopped
- 1/3 C. olive oil
- 1 tsp harissa
- sea salt
- fresh ground pepper

Directions

- Get your carrots boiling in water.
- Once the carrots are soft remove all the liquids and place them into the bowl of a food processor and add in the garlic.
- Begin to the puree the carrots and garlic then add the oil in a slow stream and continue pureeing the mix.
- Now combine in the harissa and continue to puree everything until you have a smooth paste then add in some pepper and salt.
- Stir the mix for a few secs and serve.
- Enjoy.

Amount per serving: 1

Timing Information:

Preparation	5 mins
Total Time	15 mins

Nutritional Information:

Calories	381.4
Cholesterol	0.0mg
Sodium	100.5mg
Carbohydrates	14.7g
Protein	1.5

* Percent Daily Values are based on a 2,000 calorie diet.

North African Pizza

Ingredients

- 1 pre-baked pizza crust
- 2 tsps berbere
- 1 tsp garlic, diced
- 1/4 tsp salt
- 2 tbsps olive oil
- 1 medium Chinese eggplant, sliced thick
- 1 small zucchini, sliced thick
- 1 small red onion, sliced thick
- 2 tbsps olive oil
- 1 tbsp harissa
- 1 chorizo sausage, sliced
- 6 oz. mozzarella cheese, sliced

Directions

- Set your oven to 350 degrees before doing anything else.
- Combine your olive oil with the salt, garlic, and berbere.
- Stir the mix until it is smooth and the salt has dissolved.
- Now coat your crust with the mix.
- Add your veggies to a casserole dish and top them with some olive oil and the harissa.

- Stir everything again to evenly coat the veggies and cook them in the oven for 22 mins, or until the veggies are tender.
- Let everything lose its heat then place the veggies, cheese, and sausage on the crust.
- Top the crust evenly with the ingredients and cook the pizza for 13 mins in the oven.
- Enjoy.

Amount per serving: 2

Timing Information:

Preparation	15 mins
Total Time	45 mins

Nutritional Information:

Calories	656.9
Cholesterol	93.7mg
Sodium	1202.2mg
Carbohydrates	7.9g
Protein	27.3

* Percent Daily Values are based on a 2,000 calorie diet.

Harissa Burgers

Ingredients

- 1 lb beef sausage meat
- 1 tbsp harissa
- 1 small red onion, chopped
- 1 clove garlic, crushed
- 2 tbsps flat leaf parsley, chopped
- 1 tbsp chopped chives
- 2 tbsps olive oil
- lemon slice, to serve

Directions

- Get a bowl, combine: chives, parsley, garlic, onion, harissa, and sausage.
- Work the mix with your hands then form everything into 8 balls.
- Flatten each ball into a patty and fry each patty for 6 mins per side in hot oil.
- Enjoy.

Amount per serving: 4

Timing Information:

Preparation	15 mins
Total Time	35 mins

Nutritional Information:

Calories	413.4
Cholesterol	81.6mg
Sodium	723.2mg
Carbohydrates	2.0g
Protein	17.4

* Percent Daily Values are based on a 2,000 calorie diet.

MOROCCAN STYLE COUSCOUS

Ingredients

- 14 oz. couscous
- 6 scallions, finely sliced
- 3 tbsps mint, roughly chopped
- 9 oz. cherry tomatoes, halved
- 1 3/4 C. vegetable stock, hot
- 1 tsp harissa
- 3 tbsps olive oil
- 1 lemon, juice

Directions

- Get a bowl, combine: tomatoes, couscous, mint, and scallions.
- Stir the mix to evenly distribute the ingredients.
- Now get your veggie stock boiling then combine in the harissa and stir the mix.
- Once the mix is boiling again pour it over your couscous in the bowl.
- Place a covering on the bowl and let the couscous sit for 10 mins.
- Top the mix with some lemon juice and olive oil.
- Enjoy.

Amount per serving: 10

Timing Information:

Preparation	5 mins
Total Time	10 mins

Nutritional Information:

Calories	195.4
Cholesterol	0.0mg
Sodium	7.6mg
Carbohydrates	33.7g
Protein	5.6

* Percent Daily Values are based on a 2,000 calorie diet.

ORANGE CINNAMON CHICKEN

Ingredients

- 1/4 C. harissa
- 1/2 C. orange juice
- 1 tbsp grated orange peel
- 1/4 C. cider vinegar
- 2 tbsps vegetable oil
- 2 tsps sugar
- 1 tsp ground cinnamon
- 3 lbs chicken

Directions

- Get a bowl, combine: harissa, orange juice, orange peel, vinegar, veggie oil, sugar, and cinnamon. Stir the mix until it is smooth and even.
- Coat your chicken, between the skin and meat, with some of the mix then place the pieces in a casserole dish.
- Top the chicken with the rest of the mix evenly then place a covering of plastic on the dish.
- Place everything into the fridge for 5 hrs.
- Now set your oven to 350 degrees before doing anything else.

- Remove the covering and cook the chicken in the oven for 2 hrs. Try to baste the chicken every 15 to 20 mins.
- Enjoy.

Amount per serving: 4

Timing Information:

Preparation	20 mins
Total Time	2 hrs 20 mins

Nutritional Information:

Calories	533.3
Cholesterol	155.2mg
Sodium	146.1mg
Carbohydrates	6.2g
Protein	38.7

* Percent Daily Values are based on a 2,000 calorie diet.

HARISSA SHRIMP AND CORIANDER

Ingredients

- 1/2 C. couscous
- olive oil, for frying
- 1 C. chicken stock
- 1 small onion, sliced
- 2 garlic cloves, crushed
- 1 tsp ground cumin
- 2 C. chopped tomatoes
- 1 tsp harissa
- 1/3 lb raw peeled prawns
- 1 small bunch coriander leaves

Directions

- Get a bowl, combine: 1 tsp olive oil and couscous.
- Get your stock boiling and once it is pour it over your couscous.
- Place a covering of foil on the bowl and let the mix sit for 10 mins.
- At the same time begin to stir fry your garlic and onions in 1 tbsps of oil for 3 mins then combine in the cumin,

harissa, and tomatoes, and continue to fry the mix for 60 more secs.

- Add the prawns and cook them until they are fully done for 5 mins then top everything with the coriander.
- Divide your couscous into servings and garnish each one equally with the prawn mix.
- Enjoy.

Amount per serving: 2

Timing Information:

Preparation	5 mins
Total Time	20 mins

Nutritional Information:

Calories	336.1
Cholesterol	97.5mg
Sodium	588.2mg
Carbohydrates	55.4g
Protein	21.6

* Percent Daily Values are based on a 2,000 calorie diet.

Beet Salad

(Tunisian)

Ingredients

- 2 1/2 lbs small red beets, chopped
- 2 tbsps olive oil

Dressing

- 1/2 C. green onion, diced
- 1/4 C. flat-leaf Italian parsley
- 1 garlic clove, diced
- 1 tsp harissa, to taste
- 2 tsps red wine vinegar
- salt & freshly ground black pepper

Directions

- Set your oven to 400 degrees before doing anything else.
- Get a bowl, combine: onions, parsley, garlic clove, harissa, vinegar, some pepper, and some salt. Stir the mix until it is smooth.

- Place your beets in a bowl, top them with olive oil, then place them in a casserole dish. Place a covering of foil around the dish.
- Cook the beets in the oven for 35 mins.
- Once the beets have cooled, combine them with the wet vinegar mix and toss everything.
- Enjoy warm or cold.

Amount per serving: 4

Timing Information:

Preparation	20 mins
Total Time	50 mins

Nutritional Information:

Calories	190.6
Cholesterol	0.0mg
Sodium	229.6mg
Carbohydrates	29.0g
Protein	5.1

* Percent Daily Values are based on a 2,000 calorie diet.

Punjabi Style Lentils

Ingredients

- 1 C. lentils
- 1/4 C. dry kidney beans (optional)
- water to cover
- 5 C. water
- 2 tbsp salt
- 2 tbsp vegetable oil
- 1 tbsp cumin seeds
- 4 cardamom pods
- 1 cinnamon stick, broken
- 4 bay leaves
- 6 whole cloves
- 1 1/2 tbsp ginger paste
- 1 1/2 tbsp garlic paste
- 1/2 tsp ground turmeric
- 1 pinch cayenne pepper, or more to taste
- 1 C. canned tomato puree, or more to taste
- 1 tbsp chili powder
- 2 tbsp ground coriander
- 1/4 C. butter
- 2 tbsp dried fenugreek leaves (optional)
- 1/2 C. cream (optional)

Directions

- In a large bowl, add the lentils, kidney beans and enough water to cover the lentil mixture.
- Soak for at least 2 hours or overnight, then drain well.
- In a large pan, add the lentils, kidney beans, 5 C. of the water and salt on medium heat and cook for about 1 hour, stirring occasionally.

- Remove from the heat and keep aside.
- In another pan, heat oil on medium-high heat and sauté the cumin seeds for about 12 minutes.
- Add the cardamom pods, cinnamon stick, bay leaves and cloves and sauté for about 1 minute.
- Reduce the heat to medium-low and stir in the ginger paste, garlic paste, turmeric and cayenne pepper.
- Stir in the tomato puree on medium heat and simmer for about 5 minutes.
- Add the chili powder, coriander and butter and cook, stirring till the butter is melted.
- Stir in the lentils, kidney beans and any leftover cooking water into tomato mixture and bring to a boil.
- Reduce the heat to low and stir in the fenugreek.
- Simmer, covered for about 45 minutes, stirring occasionally.
- Stir in the cream and cook and cook for about 2-4 minutes.

Amount per serving (6 total)

Timing Information:

Preparation	15 m
Cooking	2 h
Total Time	4 h 15 m

Nutritional Information:

Calories	375 kcal
Fat	21.2 g
Carbohydrates	34.2g
Protein	12.8 g
Cholesterol	48 mg
Sodium	2718 mg

* Percent Daily Values are based on a 2,000 calorie diet.

CASHEW AND CLOVE RICE

Ingredients

- 3 tbsp corn oil
- 1 onion, finely chopped
- 1 clove garlic, minced
- 1/2 C. chopped red bell pepper
- 3 whole cloves
- 1 C. long grain rice
- 4 C. water
- 1 tbsp salt
- 1 tbsp cayenne pepper
- 1 C. chopped fresh broccoli
- 1/2 C. corn kernels
- 1/2 C. fresh green beans, cut into 1 inch pieces
- 1/2 carrot, chopped
- 1/4 C. water
- 1/2 tsp ground turmeric
- 1 1/2 tbsp ground black pepper
- 1/4 C. roasted cashews
- 1/4 C. chopped fresh cilantro

Directions

- In a large pan, heat the corn oil on medium-high heat and sauté the onion, garlic, red bell pepper and whole cloves for about 10 minutes.
- Add the rice and cook, stirring continuously for about 1 minute.
- Add 4 C. of the water, salt and cayenne pepper and bring to a boil.
- Reduce the heat to medium-low and simmer, covered for about 20 minutes.

- Meanwhile in a microwave safe bowl, place the broccoli, corn, green beans, carrot, and 1/4 C. of the water and microwave, covered at full power for about 2-4 minutes.
- Gently stir in the vegetables into the rice with the turmeric, black pepper and cashews.
- Serve with a garnishing of the cilantro.

Amount per serving (4 total)

Timing Information:

Preparation	35 m
Cooking	20 m
Total Time	55 m

Nutritional Information:

Calories	374 kcal
Fat	15.3 g
Carbohydrates	54.2g
Protein	7.3 g
Cholesterol	0 mg
Sodium	1830 mg

* Percent Daily Values are based on a 2,000 calorie diet.

PANEER

(TRADITIONAL CHEESE CURRY)

Ingredients

- 1/4 C. olive oil
- 1 large yellow onion, chopped
- 1 tsp minced garlic
- 1 tsp minced fresh ginger root
- 2 serrano peppers, finely chopped
- 3/4 tsp chili powder
- 3/4 tsp ground cumin
- 3/4 tsp ground coriander
- 3/4 tsp garam masala
- 3/4 tsp ground turmeric
- 1 (14.25 oz.) can tomato puree
- 1 tbsp ketchup
- 8 oz. paneer, cubed
- 1 (16 oz.) package frozen peas, thawed
- whipping cream, to taste

Directions

- In a large pan, heat the oil on medium heat and sauté the onions till lightly browned.
- Stir in the garlic and ginger and sauté for about 1 minute.

- Reduce the heat to low and stir in the Serrano peppers and sauté for about 1 minute.
- Stir in the chili powder, cumin, coriander, garam masala and turmeric and sauté for about 1 minute.
- Add the tomato puree and ketchup and thin with the water to desired consistency.
- Stir in the paneer and peas and cook for about 2-3 minutes.
- Stir in the cream and increase the heat to medium-high.
- Bring to a rolling boil and cook for about 3-4 minutes.

Amount per serving (4 total)

Timing Information:

Preparation	30 m
Cooking	15 m
Total Time	45 m

Nutritional Information:

Calories	433 kcal
Fat	28.1 g
Carbohydrates	32.9g
Protein	15.9 g
Cholesterol	49 mg
Sodium	818 mg

* Percent Daily Values are based on a 2,000 calorie diet.

MAHARASHTRIAN STYLE VEGETABLES

Ingredients

- 4 large potatoes, finely chopped
- 1 C. cauliflower florets
- 1 carrot, finely chopped
- 1/2 C. fresh green peas
- 2 tbsp vegetable oil
- 1 large onion, chopped
- 1 tsp cumin seed
- 1 tsp black mustard seed
- 2 whole bay leaves
- 4 green chili peppers, chopped
- 3 cloves garlic, chopped
- 2 tsp minced fresh ginger root
- 1 tsp ground cumin
- 1 tsp curry powder
- 1/2 tsp chili powder (optional)
- cilantro leaves for garnish (optional)

Directions

- In a microwave-safe bowl, place the potatoes, cauliflower florets, carrot and peas.
- With a plastic wrap, cover the bowl and microwave on High for about 2 minutes.

- Remove the plastic wrap and drain the vegetables in a colander.
- In a large skillet, heat the oil and heat on medium heat and sauté the onion for about 10 minutes.
- Stir in the cumin seed, black mustard seed and bay leaves and sauté for about 30 seconds.
- Stir in the green chilis, garlic and ginger and sauté for about 1 minute.
- Stir in the ground cumin, curry powder and chili powder.
- Add the partially cooked potatoes, cauliflower, carrot and peas and cook, stirring occasionally for about 30 minutes.
- Serve with a garnishing of the cilantro leaves.

Amount per serving (6 total)

Timing Information:

Preparation	15 m
Cooking	40 m
Total Time	55 m

Nutritional Information:

Calories	279 kcal
Fat	5.3 g
Carbohydrates	53.2g
Protein	7.4 g
Cholesterol	0 mg
Sodium	48 mg

* Percent Daily Values are based on a 2,000 calorie diet.

DESI CABBAGE

Ingredients

- 2 tbsp canola oil
- 1 tsp chopped fresh ginger
- 1 serrano pepper, finely chopped
- 1 tsp caraway seed
- 1 tsp cumin seed
- 1 tsp crushed fennel seed
- 1 tsp black mustard seed
- 1 tsp fenugreek seeds
- 1 tsp ground dried turmeric
- 1/4 tsp asafoetida powder
- 5 cardamom pods
- 1/2 medium head cabbage, sliced into strips
- 1 tsp salt
- 1/4 C. water
- juice from one lime
- 1 (12 oz.) can kidney beans, garbanzo beans, or black eyed peas, drained

Directions

- In a large pan, heat the oil on medium-high heat and sauté the ginger and Serrano pepper for about 1 minute.

- Stir in the caraway, cumin, fennel, mustard, fenugreek, turmeric and asafoetida and sauté for about 20-30 seconds.
- Stir in the cardamom pods, cabbage, salt, water and lime juice and bring to a simmer.
- Simmer, covered for about 5 minutes.
- Place the beans over the cabbage, and simmer, covered for about 2 minutes.
- Uncover and simmer for about 1-2 minutes.

Amount per serving (4 total)

Timing Information:

Preparation	25 m
Cooking	15 m
Total Time	40 m

Nutritional Information:

Calories	184 kcal
Fat	8.1 g
Carbohydrates	23.3g
Protein	6.9 g
Cholesterol	0 mg
Sodium	786 mg

* Percent Daily Values are based on a 2,000 calorie diet.

BENGALI STYLE SALMON

Ingredients

- 3 tbsp mustard seed
- 5 green chili peppers, diced
- 1/4 C. vegetable oil
- 4 medium onions, chopped
- 1 tsp chili powder
- 1 tsp ground turmeric
- salt to taste
- 1/3 C. water
- 2 lb. salmon, cut into chunks

Directions

- In a bowl, add the mustard seed and chili peppers and mash till a fine paste forms.
- In a skillet, heat the oil on medium heat and sauté the onions till golden.
- Stir in the mustard paste, chili powder, turmeric, salt and water.
- Add the salmon and reduce the heat to low and simmer till most of the liquid is absorbed.

Amount per serving (6 total)

Timing Information:

Preparation	10 m
Cooking	20 m
Total Time	30 m

Nutritional Information:

Calories	435 kcal
Fat	25 g
Carbohydrates	12.8g
Protein	36.8 g
Cholesterol	98 mg
Sodium	153 mg

* Percent Daily Values are based on a 2,000 calorie diet.

ONION RELISH

Ingredients

- 1 onion, chopped
- 2 tsp ketchup
- 1 tsp lemon juice
- 1 tbsp white sugar
- 1 pinch salt
- 1 tsp chopped fresh cilantro
- 1 tsp chopped fresh fenugreek leaves
- 1 tsp chili powder

Directions

- In a medium bowl, add the onion and ketchup and mix till well combined.
- Add the lemon juice, sugar, cilantro, fenugreek and chili powder and mix till well combined.
- Refrigerate, covered to chill for about 24 hours.

Amount per serving (4 total)

Timing Information:

Preparation	5 m
Total Time	1 d 5 m

Nutritional Information:

Calories	28 kcal
Fat	0.2 g
Cholesterol	6.6g
Sodium	0.5 g
Carbohydrates	0 mg
Protein	133 mg

* Percent Daily Values are based on a 2,000 calorie diet.

ASIAN APPLE CHICKEN

Ingredients

- 2 tbsp olive oil
- 4 skinless, boneless chicken breast halves - cut into strips
- 1 large sweet onion, diced
- 2 Granny Smith apples - peeled, cored and sliced
- 1 red bell pepper, seeded and sliced into strips
- 1 tbsp red curry paste
- 1 tsp ground cinnamon
- 1/2 C. chicken broth
- 1 C. plain yogurt
- salt and pepper to taste

Directions

- In a large skillet, heat the oil on medium-high heat and stir fry the chicken for about 5-10 minutes.
- Transfer the chicken into a plate and keep aside.
- In the same skillet, add the onion and apple on medium heat and sauté for about 8 minutes.
- Add the bell pepper and cook and cook for about 5 minutes.
- Stir in the curry paste and cinnamon and cook for a few more minutes.
- Stir in the chicken broth, yogurt and cooked chicken and simmer for a few minutes till heated completely.
- Remove from the heat and stir in the salt and pepper and keep for 5 minutes before serving.

Amount per serving (4 total)

Timing Information:

Preparation	15 m
Cooking	25 m
Total Time	45 m

Nutritional Information:

Calories	305 kcal
Fat	11.6 g
Carbohydrates	19.6g
Protein	30.6 g
Cholesterol	76 mg
Sodium	181 mg

* Percent Daily Values are based on a 2,000 calorie diet.

A INDIAN STYLE SALAD

Ingredients

- 2 tbsp vegetable oil
- 1/2 small red onion, in small dice
- 1 jalapeno, seeded and minced
- 1/4 tsp ginger
- 1/4 tsp turmeric
- 1/8 tsp cayenne pepper
- 6 hard-cooked eggs, peeled and cut into large dice
- 1 small tomato, cut into small dice
- 2 tbsp chopped fresh cilantro
- Salt, to taste

Directions

- In a non-stick skillet, heat the oil on medium-high heat and sauté the onion for about 4 minutes.
- Add the jalapeño, ginger, turmeric and cayenne and sauté for about 1 minute.
- Add eggs, and cook, stirring continuously for about 2 minutes.
- Remove from the heat and stir in the tomato, cilantro and salt.
- Serve warm at room temperature or chilled.

Amount per serving (4 total)

Timing Information:

Preparation	30 m
Total Time	50 m

Nutritional Information:

Calories	187 kcal
Fat	14.9 g
Cholesterol	3g
Sodium	9.8 g
Carbohydrates	318 mg
Protein	1192 mg

* Percent Daily Values are based on a 2,000 calorie diet.

DOSAS

(PANCAKES)

Ingredients

- 1 C. brown rice flour
- 1/2 C. whole wheat flour
- 1 1/2 C. water
- 1 red onion, finely chopped
- 1 clove garlic, minced
- 1/4 C. fresh cilantro, chopped
- 1/4 tsp white sugar
- 1/2 tsp ground turmeric
- 1 tsp ground cumin
- 2 tsp whole mustard seeds
- 1 tsp cumin seeds
- 1 tsp ground coriander
- 1 tsp ground ginger
- 1 pinch cayenne pepper
- 3 tbsp rice vinegar
- 1 tbsp vegetable oil

Directions

- In a bowl, mix together the brown rice and whole wheat flours.
- Add the water and mix till a thin mixture forms.
- Add the onion, garlic, cilantro, sugar, turmeric, cumin, mustard seeds, cumin seeds, coriander, ginger, cayenne pepper and rice vinegar and mix till well combined.
- Refrigerate, covered for at least 1/2 hour or overnight.

- In a skillet, heat the oil on medium heat.
- Ass about 1/4 C. of the mixture and spread it over the bottom in a thin layer.
- Cook for about 1 minute peer side.
- Repeat with the remaining mixture.

Amount per serving (8 total)

Timing Information:

Preparation	15 m
Cooking	20 m
Total Time	1 h 5 m

Nutritional Information:

Calories	119 kcal
Fat	2.8 g
Carbohydrates	21.2g
Protein	2.9 g
Cholesterol	0 mg
Sodium	4 mg

* Percent Daily Values are based on a 2,000 calorie diet.

POT PIES INDIAN STYLE

Ingredients

Crust:

- 1/2 C. all-purpose flour
- 1/2 C. whole-wheat pastry flour
- 1/4 tsp salt
- 2 tbsp vegetable oil
- 6 tbsp ice-cold water

Filling:

- 1 1/4 lb. potatoes, peeled and quartered
- 1 tbsp black mustard seeds
- 1 tsp curry powder
- 1 tsp ground ginger
- 1/2 tsp ground cumin
- 1/8 tsp red pepper flakes (optional)
- 1 1/2 tsp vegetable oil
- 1 C. diced onion
- 1/2 C. diced carrot
- 1 tbsp minced garlic
- 1 C. low-sodium vegetable broth
- 1 C. frozen peas
- 2 tsp white sugar
- salt and ground black pepper to taste
- 2 tbsp milk

Directions

- Set your oven to 375 degrees F before doing anything else.
- In a bowl, mix together the all-purpose flour, pastry flour and salt.
- Add 2 tbsp of the vegetable oil in the flour mixture, stirring till clumps form.

- Stir cold water, 1 tbsp at a time in the dough till it holds together
- Make a ball from the dough.
- With a damp towel, cover and keep aside.
- In a large pan of salted water, add the potatoes and bring to a boil.
- Reduce the heat to medium-low and simmer for about 15 minutes.
- Drain well.
- Transfer the drained potatoes into a large bowl and mash till only small chunks remain.
- Add the mustard seeds, curry powder, ground ginger, cumin and red pepper flakes and stir to combine.
- In a skillet, heat 1 1/2 tsp of the vegetable oil on medium heat and sauté the onion, carrot and garlic for about 5 minutes.
- With a spoon, move the onion mixture to one side of the skillet.
- Add the seasoning mixture to the skillet and sauté for about 30 seconds.
- Stir the onion mixture with the spice mixture.
- Stir in the vegetable broth and peas.
- Fold the carrot mixture into the mashed potatoes.
- Add the sugar, salt and pepper and stir to combine.
- Spread the filling mixture into a 9-inch pie dish.
- Place the dough out onto a lightly floured smooth surface and roll into an 11-inch disc.
- Place the dough over the pie filling and press down on the dough in several spots to remove any pockets of the air.
- Trim the excess dough from the edges and with your fingers, crimp the edges of the dough.

- Carefully, cut a large cross in the center of the dough to vent the steam and brush the top of the dough with the milk.
- Cook in the oven for about 40-50 minutes.
- Cool the pie for about 5 minutes before serving.

Amount per serving (6 total)

Timing Information:

Preparation	20 m
Cooking	1 h
Total Time	1 h 25 m

Nutritional Information:

Calories	248 kcal
Fat	6.9 g
Carbohydrates	41.3g
Protein	6.5 g
Cholesterol	1 mg
Sodium	176 mg

* Percent Daily Values are based on a 2,000 calorie diet.

MUMBAI BREAKFAST

Ingredients

- 1 tsp oil, or as needed
- 2 medium eggs
- 1/2 C. heavy whipping cream
- 1/4 clove garlic, minced
- 1/4 C. shredded Cheddar cheese, or more to taste
- 2 tsp curry powder
- 1 tsp ground cumin (optional)

Directions

- In a skillet, heat the oil on medium-high heat.
- In a bowl, add the eggs and cream and beat well.
- Add the garlic, Cheddar cheese, curry powder and cumin and stir to combine.
- Add the egg mixture in the hot oil and cook, stirring for about 5 minutes.

Amount per serving (2 total)

Timing Information:

Preparation	10 m
Cooking	5 m
Total Time	15 m

Nutritional Information:

Calories	377 kcal
Fat	35.5 g
Carbohydrates	4g
Protein	12.3 g
Cholesterol	286 mg
Sodium	203 mg

* Percent Daily Values are based on a 2,000 calorie diet.

Chennai Style Rice Pilaf

Ingredients

- 1/4 C. water
- 1 (14.5 oz.) can chicken broth
- 1 C. long grain rice
- 1 tsp curry powder
- 1/2 tsp garlic powder
- 1/4 tsp ground cinnamon
- 1/8 tsp paprika
- 2 pinches ground cloves
- 1 small onion, coarsely chopped

Directions

- In a pan, add the water and chicken broth and bring to a boil.
- In a bowl, mix together the rice, curry powder, garlic powder, cinnamon, paprika and cloves.
- Add spiced rice and onion to the boiling broth and cook, covered for about 20-25 minutes.

Amount per serving (4 total)

Timing Information:

Preparation	10 m
Cooking	20 m
Total Time	30 m

Nutritional Information:

Calories	188 kcal
Fat	0.7 g
Carbohydrates	40.1g
Protein	4.1 g
Cholesterol	2 mg
Sodium	440 mg

* Percent Daily Values are based on a 2,000 calorie diet.

SHRIMP ANDHRA

Ingredients

- 2 tsp paprika
- 1 tsp ground cumin
- 2 tsp ground turmeric
- 1/2 tsp salt
- 1/2 onion, minced
- 1 lb. uncooked medium shrimp, peeled and deveined
- 2 tbsp vegetable oil
- 1/2 tsp mustard seed
- 1 tbsp garlic paste
- 3/4 tsp ginger paste
- 1 tbsp water
- 1 tomato, diced
- 1 large green bell pepper, cut into 1-inch squares
- 1/2 tsp ground black pepper (optional)
- 1 tsp lemon juice (optional)

Directions

- In a large bowl, place the shrimp.
- In a small bowl, mix together the paprika, cumin, turmeric, and salt.
- Place about 3/4 the of the spice mixture over the shrimp and keep aside for about 10 minutes.
- With a mortar and pestle, crush the onion slightly.
- In a frying pan, heat the oil on high heat and sauté the mustard seeds for about 1-2 minutes.
- Reduce the heat to medium-high and sauté the onion, garlic paste and ginger paste for about 10-15 minutes.
- Add the water in the remaining spice mixture and stir to combine.

- Transfer the spice mixture in the pan and stir to combine.
- Stir in the tomatoes and cook for about 5 minutes.
- Stir in the green peppers and cook for about 1-2 minutes.
- Reduce the heat to medium and stir in the shrimp and cook for about 3-5 minutes.
- Increase the heat to medium-high and cook till all the liquid is absorbed.
- Remove from the heat and sprinkle with the black pepper.
- Serve with a drizzling of the lemon juice.

Amount per serving (4 total)

Timing Information:

Preparation	20 m
Cooking	30 m
Total Time	1 h

Nutritional Information:

Calories	191 kcal
Fat	8.5 g
Carbohydrates	7.1g
Protein	19.9 g
Cholesterol	173 mg
Sodium	622 mg

* Percent Daily Values are based on a 2,000 calorie diet.

MEDITERRANEAN ASIAN STOVETOP LAMB

Ingredients

- 3 tbsp canola oil
- 1 onion, finely chopped
- 4 cloves garlic, crushed
- 1/2 tsp cumin seeds, or to taste
- 1 lb. lamb stew meat, cubed
- 3 tbsp tomato paste
- 2 tsp ground coriander
- 2 tsp salt, or to taste
- 2 tsp garam masala
- 1 1/2 tsp ground turmeric
- 1 tsp red chili powder, or to taste

Directions

- In a pan, heat the canola oil on medium heat and sauté the onion, garlic and cumin seeds for about 10-15 minutes.
- Stir in the lamb, tomato paste, coriander, salt, garam masala, turmeric and red chili powder.
- Simmer, covered for about 1 hour.

Amount per serving (4 total)

Timing Information:

Preparation	15 m
Cooking	1 h 10 m
Total Time	1 h 25 m

Nutritional Information:

Calories	242 kcal
Fat	15.6 g
Carbohydrates	8.1g
Protein	18.1 g
Cholesterol	53 mg
Sodium	1305 mg

* Percent Daily Values are based on a 2,000 calorie diet.

MOROCCAN TAGINE

Ingredients

- 1 tbsp olive oil
- 2 skinless, boneless chicken breast halves - cut into chunks
- 1/2 onion, chopped
- 3 cloves garlic, minced
- 1 small butternut squash, peeled and chopped
- 1 (15.5 ounce) can garbanzo beans, drained and rinsed
- 1 carrot, peeled and chopped
- 1 (14.5 ounce) can diced tomatoes with juice
- 1 (14 ounce) can vegetable broth
- 1 tbsp sugar
- 1 tbsp lemon juice
- 1 tsp salt
- 1 tsp ground coriander
- 1 dash cayenne pepper

Directions

- Cook onion, garlic and chicken over hot olive oil in a pan for about 15 minutes or until you see that it is brown.
- Now put squash, carrot, tomatoes, garbanzo beans, broth, sugar, and lemon into it before adding some salt, cayenne pepper and coriander for taste.
- Bring all this to boil before cooking it over low heat for about 30 minutes or until the vegetables are tender.

Serving: 6

Timing Information:

Preparation	Cooking	Total Time
2 hrs	20 mins	2 hrs 20 mins

Nutritional Information:

Calories	265 kcal
Carbohydrates	44.7 g
Cholesterol	20 mg
Fat	4.3 g
Fiber	8.1 g
Protein	14.1 g
Sodium	878 mg

* Percent Daily Values are based on a 2,000 calorie diet.

MOROCCAN CHICKEN

Ingredients

- 1 pound skinless, boneless chicken breast meat - cubed
- 2 tsps salt
- 1 onion, chopped
- 2 cloves garlic, chopped
- 2 carrots, sliced
- 2 stalks celery, sliced
- 1 tbsp minced fresh ginger root
- 1/2 tsp paprika
- 3/4 tsp ground cumin
- 1/2 tsp dried oregano
- 1/4 tsp ground cayenne pepper
- 1/4 tsp ground turmeric
- 1 1/2 C. chicken broth
- 1 C. crushed tomatoes
- 1 C. canned chickpeas, drained
- 1 zucchini, sliced
- 1 tbsp lemon juice

Directions

- Cook chicken in a pan after adding salt and brown in it until you see that is cooked through.
- Using the same pan; cook celery, garlic, onion and carrot before adding ginger, turmeric, cayenne pepper, paprika, cumin and oregano into it.
- Add broth as well as tomatoes after cooking it for one minute.

- Now put the cooked chicken into this pan and cook it over low heat for 10 minutes.
- At last, put chickpeas and zucchini into the pan and cook it for about 15 minutes or until tender.
- Pour some lemon juice over everything before serving.

Serving: 4

Timing Information:

Preparation	Cooking	Total Time
10 mins	30 mins	45 mins

Nutritional Information:

Calories	286 kcal
Carbohydrates	27.9 g
Cholesterol	67 mg
Fat	3.7 g
Fiber	6.3 g
Protein	36 g
Sodium	2128 mg

* Percent Daily Values are based on a 2,000 calorie diet.

MOROCCAN INSPIRED YAM STEW

Ingredients
- 2 tbsps olive oil
- 3 C. chopped yams
- 2 large onions, chopped
- 2 C. chopped cabbage
- 2 tomatoes, chopped
- 6 tbsps flaked coconut
- 3 cloves garlic, minced
- 3 C. tomato juice
- 1 C. apple juice
- 1 tsp ground ginger
- 1/4 tsp cayenne pepper
- 1 pinch salt
- 1 large green bell pepper, chopped
- 1/2 C. peanut butter

Directions
- Cook garlic, tomatoes, onions, cabbage, yams and coconut in hot oil for about 10 minutes.
- Add some apple juice, ginger, salt, cayenne pepper and tomato juice into the vegetables and cook this for another 1 hour at medium heat.
- Now add some peanut butter and bell pepper into this mixture, and cook all this for another 30 minutes to melt down the peanut butter.
- Serve.

Serving: 6

Timing Information:

Preparation	Cooking	Total Time
15 mins	20 mins	35 mins

Nutritional Information:

Calories	379 kcal
Carbohydrates	46.8 g
Cholesterol	0 mg
Fat	19.6 g
Fiber	8.6 g
Protein	9.6 g
Sodium	447 mg

* Percent Daily Values are based on a 2,000 calorie diet.

MOROCCAN TAGINE II

Ingredients

- 1 tbsp olive oil
- 2 large onions, peeled and sliced into rings
- 2 pounds lamb meat, cut into 1 1/2 inch cubes
- 1 tsp ground cumin
- 1 tsp ground coriander seed
- 1 tsp ground ginger
- 1 tsp ground cinnamon
- salt to taste
- 1 tsp ground black pepper
- 4 pears - peeled, cored and cut into 1 1/2 inch chunks
- 1/2 C. golden raisins
- 1/2 C. blanched slivered almonds

Directions

- Cook onion in hot oil before adding lamb meat and cooking it until brown.
- Add cinnamon, cumin, salt, coriander, pepper and ginger into it before pouring in enough water to cover the meat.
- Now cook it covered for two full hours.
- Now add almonds, pears and golden raisins into it before cooking it for another 5 minutes.
- Serve.

Serving: 4

Timing Information:

Preparation	Cooking	Total Time
15 mins	2 hr	2 hrs 15 mins

Nutritional Information:

Calories	394 kcal
Carbohydrates	42.7 g
Cholesterol	71 mg
Fat	14.5 g
Fiber	7.5 g
Protein	26.4 g
Sodium	68 mg

* Percent Daily Values are based on a 2,000 calorie diet.

MOROCCAN CHICKPEA STEW

Ingredients

- 1 tbsp olive oil
- 1 small onion, chopped
- 2 cloves garlic, minced
- 2 tsps ground cumin
- 2 tsps ground coriander
- 1/2 tsp cayenne pepper, or to taste
- 1 tsp garam masala
- 1/2 tsp curry powder
- 1 pinch salt
- 3 potatoes, cut into 1/2-inch cubes
- 1 (14.5 ounce) can diced tomatoes, undrained
- 1 C. tomato sauce
- 1 C. golden raisins
- water, or enough to cover
- 1 (14.5 ounce) can chickpeas, drained and rinsed
- 1 bunch kale, ribs removed, chopped
- 1/2 C. chopped fresh cilantro

Directions

- Cook onions and garlic in hot oil for about 7 minutes before adding garam masala, salt, cayenne pepper and curry powder into it.

- Cook for another one minute before adding potatoes, raisins, tomato sauce and some finely sliced tomatoes into it.
- Pour water into everything before cooking it over medium heat for 15 more minutes.
- Now add chickpeas and kale into this mixture, and cook it over low heat for an additional three minutes.
- Sprinkle some cilantro over this prepared stew before serving.

Serving: 4

Timing Information:

Preparation	Cooking	Total Time
15 hrs	25 mins	40 mins

Nutritional Information:

Calories	476 kcal
Carbohydrates	96.1 g
Cholesterol	0 mg
Fat	6.5 g
Fiber	13.6 g
Protein	15.7 g
Sodium	1263 mg

* Percent Daily Values are based on a 2,000 calorie diet.

Moroccan Potato Bean Soup

Ingredients

- 6 C. water
- 1 (15 ounce) can kidney beans
- 3 tbsps olive oil
- 2 onions, chopped
- 2 potatoes, peeled and cubed
- 3 tbsps chicken bouillon powder
- 1/2 tsp ground turmeric
- 1/2 tsp ground black pepper
- 1/2 tsp ground white pepper
- 1/2 tsp cayenne pepper(optional)
- 2 tsps curry powder
- 2 tbsps soy sauce
- 1/2 C. whole milk
- 1/2 C. half-and-half
- 1/2 C. dry potato flakes
- 1/4 C. chopped green onions

Directions

- Bring the mixture of white beans and water to a boil before turning the heat down to low and cooking it for another 15 minutes.
- Now cook onions in hot olive oil until brown.
- Put potatoes, fried onions, turmeric, black pepper, chicken soup base, cayenne pepper, curry powder, white

pepper, and soy sauce into the beans, and cook for another 15 minutes or until you see that the potatoes are tender.

- At last, put whole milk, half and half cream, and instant potato flakes into it before bringing all this back to boil.
- You can garnish this soup with green onions and some chopped chives.
- Serve.

Serving: 8

Timing Information:

Preparation	Cooking	Total Time
15 min	45 mins	1 hr

Nutritional Information:

Calories	198 kcal
Carbohydrates	25.9 g
Cholesterol	8 mg
Fat	8.1 g
Fiber	5.5 g
Protein	6.7 g
Sodium	1167 mg

* Percent Daily Values are based on a 2,000 calorie diet.

QUICK MOROCCAN COUSCOUS

Ingredients

- 2 C. water
- 1 C. pearl (Israeli) couscous
- 1 tbsp olive oil
- 1/2 C. chopped yellow onion
- 1 shallot, chopped
- 6 cloves garlic, quartered
- 1/2 C. golden raisins
- 1/2 C. chopped oil-packed sun-dried tomatoes
- 1/2 C. slivered almonds
- 1/2 tsp kosher salt
- 1/4 tsp ground black pepper
- 3 tbsps lemon juice
- 1 tbsp butter, softened

Directions

- Add couscous into the boiling hot water and cook this for about 15 minutes or until all the water is absorbed the couscous that you have added.
- Cook onion, shallot and garlic in hot oil for about 20 minutes before adding tomatoes and almonds, and cooking it for five more minutes.
- Now add cooked couscous into it and cook it for five minutes before adding salt, lemon juice and pepper for taste. Combine some butter before serving.

Serving: 8

Timing Information:

Preparation	Cooking	Total Time
10 min	35 mins	45 min

Nutritional Information:

Calories	265 kcal
Carbohydrates	38.6 g
Cholesterol	5 mg
Fat	10.3 g
Fiber	3.6 g
Protein	6.6 g
Sodium	208 mg

* Percent Daily Values are based on a 2,000 calorie diet.

Moroccan Meat Pie

Ingredients

- 1 sweet potato, diced
- 1 1/4 C. water
- 1/4 yellow onion, chopped
- 3 cloves garlic, minced
- 1 (.87 ounce) package dry brown gravy mix
- 1/2 tsp ground cumin
- 1/2 tsp ground cinnamon
- 1/2 tsp curry powder
- 1/2 tsp ground ginger
- 1/2 tsp ground black pepper
- 1/2 tsp ground turmeric
- 1/2 tsp salt
- 1 C. shredded leftover pot roast
- 1/2 C. peas
- 1/2 C. frozen corn
- 1 frozen deep-dish pie crust
- 1/2 C. crumbled feta cheese

Directions

- Set your oven at 400 degrees F before doing anything else.
- Cook sweet potato in boiling water for about 15 minutes at medium heat.
- Now bring the mixture of onion, garlic and water to boil, and after turning the heat down to low, cook for five minutes or until the onion softens up.

- Now add gravy mix, cumin, peas, ginger, black pepper, turmeric, salt leftover pot, cinnamon, roast, sweet potatoes, curry powder and corn into the pan, and cook for five minutes before pouring this into the pie crust.
- Put some cheese over it before baking it for about 25 minutes or until the top start to turn golden brown in color.

Serving: 4

Timing Information:

Preparation	Cooking	Total Time
20 min	50 mins	1 hr 10 mins

Nutritional Information:

Calories	569 kcal
Carbohydrates	49.2 g
Cholesterol	65 mg
Fat	31.6 g
Fiber	6 g
Protein	22.6 g
Sodium	1159 mg

* Percent Daily Values are based on a 2,000 calorie diet.

Moroccan Peach Roasted Chicken

Ingredients

- 1/4 C. margarine or butter
- 1/4 C. honey
- 1 tsp rose water
- 1 tsp salt
- ground black pepper to taste

- 4 pounds bone-in chicken pieces, with skin
- 1 pound fresh peaches, pitted and sliced
- 1 tbsp white sugar
- 1/2 C. toasted slivered almonds (optional)

Directions

- Set your oven at 425 degrees F before doing anything else.
- Heat the mixture of margarine, pepper, honey, salt and rose water in the microwave for about 30 seconds to melt down the margarine.
- Now pour this mixture over chicken in a baking dish and mix it well.
- Bake this in the preheated oven for about 15 minutes before turning the temperature down to 350 degrees F and baking it for another 20 minutes after adding peaches and sugar into it.
- Place chicken in a serving dish of your choice. Serve.

Serving: 6

Timing Information:

Preparation	Cooking	Total Time
20 min	30 mins	50 mins

Nutritional Information:

Calories	567 kcal
Carbohydrates	19.1 g
Cholesterol	130 mg
Fat	34.9 g
Fiber	0.9 g
Protein	42.9 g
Sodium	603 mg

* Percent Daily Values are based on a 2,000 calorie diet.

Spanish Moroccan Fish

Ingredients

- 1 tbsp vegetable oil
- 1 medium onion, chopped
- 1 clove garlic, finely chopped
- 2 red bell pepper, seeded and sliced into strips
- 1 large carrot, thinly sliced
- 3 tomatoes, chopped
- 4 olives, chopped
- 1 (15 ounce) can garbanzo beans, drained and rinsed
- 1/4 C. fresh parsley, chopped
- 3 tbsps paprika
- 4 tbsps ground cumin
- 1 tsp cayenne pepper
- 2 tbsps chicken bouillon granules
- Salt to taste
- 5 pounds tilapia fillets

Directions

- Cook onion and garlic in hot oil for about five minutes before adding bell peppers, carrots, garbanzo beans, tomatoes and olives, and cook for five more minutes.
- Now add chicken bouillon, parsley, cayenne, paprika, salt and cumin before adding fish on top of all this and enough water to cover the vegetables.

- Turn the heat down to low and cook for another 40 minutes.
- Serve.

Serving: 6

Timing Information:

Preparation	Cooking	Total Time
30 min	1 hr	1 hr 30 mins

Nutritional Information:

Calories	529 kcal
Carbohydrates	23.4 g
Cholesterol	139 mg
Fat	10.2 g
Fiber	6.4 g
Protein	83.2 g
Sodium	736 mg

* Percent Daily Values are based on a 2,000 calorie diet.

SWEET AND NUTTY MOROCCAN COUSCOUS

Ingredients

- 2 C. vegetable broth
- 5 tbsps unsalted butter
- 1/3 C. chopped dates
- 1/3 C. chopped dried apricots
- 1/3 C. golden raisins
- 2 C. dry couscous
- 3 tsps ground cinnamon
- 1/2 C. slivered almonds, toasted

Directions

- Bring the vegetable broth to boil before adding butter, raisins, apricots and dates into it, and boiling it for three full minutes.
- Combine this with couscous after turning off the heat and then let it stand covered for about 5 minutes.
- Just before you serve, add cinnamon and toasted almonds.
- Enjoy.

Serving: 6

Timing Information:

Preparation	Cooking	Total Time
15 min	5 mins	20 mins

Nutritional Information:

Calories	442 kcal
Carbohydrates	68.2 g
Cholesterol	25 mg
Fat	14.8 g
Fiber	6.4 g
Protein	10.5 g
Sodium	164 mg

* Percent Daily Values are based on a 2,000 calorie diet.

TEMPEH KABOBS WITH MOROCCAN COUSCOUS

Ingredients

- 2 pounds ground lamb
- 1 C. raisins
- 5 ounces goat cheese
- 1/3 C. mayonnaise
- 1 red onion, finely chopped
- 2 cloves garlic, finely chopped
- 2 tbsps chopped fresh cilantro
- 3/4 tbsp ground cayenne pepper
- 1/2 tsp ground cumin
- 1/2 tsp ground coriander
- salt to taste
- coarsely ground black pepper to taste

Directions

- At first you need to set a grill or grilling plate to medium heat and put some oil before starting anything else.
- Combine ground lamb, ground coriander, raisins, mayonnaise, red onion, garlic, cilantro, goat cheese,

cayenne pepper, cumin, salt and black pepper in a bowl of your choice.

- Divide this evenly into six even portions and pierce this into skewers.
- Put these on the preheated grill and cook it for about 4 minutes each side or until you see that the cheese has melted completely.
- Serve.

NOTE: If using a grilling plate instead of grill, then adjust the cooking time of the meat so that everything is fully cooked through.

Serving: 6

Timing Information:

Preparation	Cooking	Total Time
20 mins	10 mins	30 mins

Nutritional Information:

Calories	554 kcal
Carbohydrates	22.7 g
Cholesterol	125 mg
Fat	37.6 g
Fiber	1.5 g
Protein	32.2 g
Sodium	280 mg

* Percent Daily Values are based on a 2,000 calorie diet.

Moroccan Mashed Potatoes

Ingredients

- 10 large baking potatoes, peeled and cubed
- 3 tbsps olive oil, or as needed
- 1 onion, diced
- 1 tbsp ground turmeric
- 1 tbsp salt, or to taste
- 2 tsps ground black pepper
- 1/2 tsp ground cumin

Directions

- Place potatoes in boiling water and cook until tender, about twenty minutes.
- Cook onion in hot oil for about six minutes or until lightly browned.
- Add this to the potatoes after draining water and mash before adding turmeric, cumin, pepper and salt into.
- Add two tbsps of olive oil to make these potatoes a little creamy.
- Serve.

Serving: 32

Timing Information:

Preparation	Cooking	Total Time
16 mins	20 mins	36 mins

Nutritional Information:

Calories	103 kcal
Carbohydrates	21.3 g
Cholesterol	0 mg
Fat	1.4 g
Fiber	2 g
Protein	1.8 g
Sodium	224 mg

* Percent Daily Values are based on a 2,000 calorie diet.

MOROCCAN SHABBAT FISH

Ingredients

- 1 red bell pepper, cut into thin strips
- 3 tomatoes, sliced
- 6 (6 ounce) tilapia fillets
- 2 tbsps paprika
- 1 tbsp chicken bouillon granules
- 1 tsp cayenne pepper
- salt and pepper to taste
- 1/4 C. olive oil
- 1 C. water
- 1/4 C. chopped fresh parsley

Directions

- Set your oven at 200 degrees F before doing anything else.
- Put red peppers and sliced tomatoes in the baking dish and add tilapia fillets on top of it.
- Add mixture of paprika, cayenne, salt, pepper, chicken bouillon, olive oil and water over fish in the baking dish.
- Bake this for one full hour in the preheated oven after covering the baking dish with aluminum foil.

Serving: 6

Timing Information:

Preparation	Cooking	Total Time
20 mins	1 hr	1 hr 20 mins

Nutritional Information:

Calories	278 kcal
Carbohydrates	5.9 g
Cholesterol	62 mg
Fat	12 g
Fiber	2.3 g
Protein	35.9 g
Sodium	303 mg

* Percent Daily Values are based on a 2,000 calorie diet.

Moroccan Ksra (Flatbread)

Ingredients

- 7/8 C. water
- 2 1/4 C. bread flour
- 3/4 C. semolina flour
- 1 tsp anise seed
- 1 1/2 tsps salt
- 1/2 tsp white sugar
- 2 tsps active dry yeast
- 1 tbsp olive oil
- 1 tbsp sesame seeds(optional)

Directions

- Put all the ingredients of the into a bread machine by following the order that has been recommended by its manufacture.
- Start the machine after selecting the dough cycle.
- When it is done, cut this into two parts before shaping some balls out of it.
- Flatten these balls out and place them on a baking dish that is lightly floured.
- Now let it stand as it is for about 30 minutes while covered.

- Set the heat of your oven to 400 degrees F and brush each and every loaf with some olive oil and sesame seeds.
- Bake this for about 25 minutes in the oven or until you see that it is golden brown.

Serving: 2

Timing Information:

Preparation	Cooking	Total Time
2 hrs	20 mins	2 hrs 20 mins

Nutritional Information:

Calories	278 kcal
Carbohydrates	5.9 g
Cholesterol	62 mg
Fat	12 g
Fiber	2.3 g
Protein	35.9 g
Sodium	303 mg

* Percent Daily Values are based on a 2,000 calorie diet.

Fava Bean Breakfast Spread

Ingredients

- 1 (15 ounce) can fava beans
- 1 1/2 tbsps olive oil
- 1 large onion, chopped
- 1 large tomato, diced
- 1 tsp ground cumin
- 1/4 C. chopped fresh parsley
- 1/4 C. fresh lemon juice
- salt and pepper to taste
- ground red pepper, to taste

Directions

- Bring beans to boil and then add onion, olive oil, parsley, salt, red pepper, cumin, tomato and pepper into it.
- Boil the mixture again and cook it for another 5 minutes at medium heat.
- Serve it with grilled pita

Serving: 6

Timing Information:

Preparation	Cooking	Total Time
10 mins	10 mins	20 mins

Nutritional Information:

Calories	101 kcal
Carbohydrates	13.6 g
Cholesterol	0 mg
Fat	3.7 g
Fiber	3.5 g
Protein	4.6 g
Sodium	322 mg

* Percent Daily Values are based on a 2,000 calorie diet.

Moroccan Peanut Stew

Ingredients
- 2 tbsps peanut oil
- 1 red onion, chopped
- 2 cloves garlic, minced
- 2 tbsps chopped fresh ginger
- 1 pound chicken, cut into chunks (optional)
- 1 tbsp crushed red pepper, or to taste
- salt and ground black pepper to taste
- 5 C. chicken stock
- 3 small sweet potatoes, cut into chunks
- 1 (16 ounce) can chopped tomatoes, with liquid
- 1/4 pound collard greens, roughly chopped
- 1 C. chunky peanut butter

Directions
- Cook ginger, onion and garlic in hot peanut oil at medium heat for 5 minutes and then add chicken and cook until brown.
- Add some red pepper, pepper and salt according to your taste and then add chicken stock and some sweet potatoes into it and cook it for another 15 minutes before serving.

Serving: 4

Timing Information:

Preparation	Cooking	Total Time
20 mins	45 mins	1 hr 5 mins

Nutritional Information:

Calories	731 kcal
Carbohydrates	44.9 g
Cholesterol	70 mg
Fat	43.8 g
Fiber	11.1 g
Protein	45.5 g
Sodium	1470 mg

* Percent Daily Values are based on a 2,000 calorie diet.

Moroccan Yam Soup

Ingredients
- 1 tsp vegetable oil
- 1 small onion, chopped
- 1 large sweet potato, peeled and diced
- 1 clove garlic, minced
- 4 C. chicken broth
- 1 tsp dried thyme
- 1/2 tsp ground cumin
- 1 C. chunky salsa
- 1 (15.5 ounce) can garbanzo beans, drained
- 1 C. diced zucchini
- 1/2 C. cooked rice
- 2 tbsps creamy peanut butter

Directions
- Cook sweet potato, garlic and onion in hot oil and then add chicken broth, cumin and thyme.
- Cook it for 15 minutes and then add garbanzo beans, salsa and zucchini into it and cook for another 15 minutes at low heat.
- Now add cooked rice and peanut butter into it and mix it until peanut butter has dissolved.
- Serve with pita chips and salad.

Serving: 4

Timing Information:

Preparation	Cooking	Total Time
10 mins	30 mins	40 mins

Nutritional Information:

Calories	345 kcal
Carbohydrates	62.2 g
Cholesterol	0 mg
Fat	6.9 g
Fiber	10.7 g
Protein	11.5 g
Sodium	822 mg

* Percent Daily Values are based on a 2,000 calorie diet.

MEDITERRANEAN PASTA

Ingredients

- 1 (16 oz.) package penne pasta
- 1 1/2 tbsps butter
- 1/2 C. chopped red onion
- 2 cloves garlic, minced
- 1 lb. skinless, boneless chicken breast halves - cut into bite-size pieces
- 1 (14 oz.) can artichoke hearts in water
- 1 tomato, chopped
- 1/2 C. crumbled feta cheese
- 3 tbsps chopped fresh parsley
- 2 tbsps lemon juice
- 1 tsp dried oregano
- salt to taste
- ground black pepper to taste

Directions

- Boil your pasta in water and salt for 9 mins then remove all the liquids.

- At the same time, stir fry your garlic and onions in butter for 4 mins, then combine in the chicken, and cook everything for 9 more mins.
- Set the heat to a low level and add in your artichokes after chopping them and discarding their liquids.
- Cook this mix for 3 more mins before adding in: pasta, tomatoes, oregano, feta, lemon juice, and the fresh parsley.
- Cook everything for 4 mins to get it all hot. Then add in your pepper and salt after shutting the heat.
- Enjoy.

Amount per serving (4 total)

Timing Information:

Preparation	20 m
Cooking	30 m
Total Time	50 m

Nutritional Information:

Calories	685 kcal
Fat	13.2 g
Carbohydrates	96.2g
Protein	47 g
Cholesterol	94 mg
Sodium	826 mg

* Percent Daily Values are based on a 2,000 calorie diet.

CLASSICAL HUMMUS III
(BLACK BEAN)

Ingredients

- 1 clove garlic
- 1 (15 oz.) can black beans; drain and reserve liquid
- 2 tbsps lemon juice
- 1 1/2 tbsps tahini
- 3/4 tsp ground cumin
- 1/2 tsp salt
- 1/4 tsp cayenne pepper
- 1/4 tsp paprika
- 10 Greek olives

Directions

- Blend your garlic in a blender with a few pulses to mince it then add in: half of your cayenne, black beans, salt, 2 tbsps of black bean juice, half tsp cumin, tahini, and lemon juice.
- Blend this mix until it has the consistency of hummus.
- Add everything to a bowl and top it all with olives and paprika.
- Enjoy.

Amount per serving (8 total)

Timing Information:

Preparation	
Cooking	5 m
Total Time	5 m

Nutritional Information:

Calories	81 kcal
Fat	3.1 g
Carbohydrates	10.3g
Protein	3.9 g
Cholesterol	0 mg
Sodium	427 mg

* Percent Daily Values are based on a 2,000 calorie diet.

GREEK SPINACH PUFF PASTRY BAKE

Ingredients

- 3 tbsps olive oil
- 1 large onion, chopped
- 1 bunch green onions, chopped
- 2 cloves garlic, minced
- 2 lbs spinach, rinsed and chopped
- 1/2 C. chopped fresh parsley
- 2 eggs, lightly beaten
- 1/2 C. ricotta cheese
- 1 C. crumbled feta cheese
- 8 sheets phyllo dough
- 1/4 C. olive oil

Directions

- Coat a baking pan with nonstick spray and then set your oven to 350 degrees before doing anything else.
- Stir fry your garlic, onions, and green onions in olive oil for 4 mins. Then add in, the parsley and the spinach, and cook it all for 3 more mins.
- Remove all the contents.
- Get a bowl, combine: feta, onion mix, ricotta, and eggs.

- Coat a piece of phyllo with olive oil then layer it in the pan.
- Add another piece and also more olive oil.
- Do this two more times.
- Add your ricotta mix and fold the phyllo around the filling and seal it.
- Cook everything in the oven for 35 mins.
- Then cut the contents into your preferred shape.
- Enjoy.

Amount per serving (5 total)

Timing Information:

Preparation	30 m
Cooking	1 h
Total Time	1 h 30 m

Nutritional Information:

Calories	528 kcal
Fat	36.7 g
Carbohydrates	32.8g
Protein	21 g
Cholesterol	108 mg
Sodium	925 mg

* Percent Daily Values are based on a 2,000 calorie diet.

Souvlaki III

Ingredients

Marinade:

- 3/4 C. balsamic vinaigrette salad dressing
- 3 tbsps lemon juice
- 1 tbsp dried oregano
- 1/2 tsp freshly ground black pepper
- 4 skinless, boneless chicken breast halves

White Sauce:

- 1/2 C. seeded, shredded cucumber
- 1 tsp kosher salt
- 1 C. plain yogurt
- 1/4 C. sour cream
- 1 tbsp lemon juice
- 1/2 tbsp rice vinegar
- 1 tsp olive oil

- 1 clove garlic, minced
- 1 tbsp chopped fresh dill
- 1/2 tsp Greek seasoning
- kosher salt to taste
- freshly ground black pepper to taste
- 4 large pita bread rounds
- 1 heart of romaine lettuce, cut into 1/4 inch slices
- 1 red onion, thinly sliced
- 1 tomato, halved and sliced
- 1/2 C. kalamata olives
- 1/2 C. pepperoncini
- 1 C. crumbled feta cheese

Directions

- Get a bowl, combine: chicken, black pepper (1/2 tsp), balsamic, oregano, and the juice of half of a lemon.
- Place a covering on the bowl and place the contents in the fridge for 2 hrs.
- Get a 2nd bowl and add in your cucumbers after shredding them and also some kosher salt.
- Let this stand for 10 mins.
- Get a 3rd bowl, combine: olive oil, garlic, yogurt, dill, rice vinegar, Greek seasoning, sour cream, and 1 tbsp of lemon juice.
- Place this mix in the fridge.
- Now grill your chicken pieces for 9 mins then flip them and cook the chicken pieces for 9 more mins.
- Let the chicken cool and then julienne it.
- Grill your pieces of pita for 3 mins and flip them throughout the entire grilling time.
- Fill each piece of pita with: pepperoncini, chicken, olive, lettuce, tomato, and onions.
- Add a topping of white sauce from the fridge and some feta on the side.
- Enjoy.

Amount per serving (4 total)

Timing Information:

Preparation	30 m
Cooking	20 m
Total Time	1 h 50 m

Nutritional Information:

Calories	764 kcal
Fat	40.5 g
Carbohydrates	55.9g
Protein	44.4 g
Cholesterol	133 mg
Sodium	3170 mg

* Percent Daily Values are based on a 2,000 calorie diet.

PENNE CANNELLINI AND TOMATOES SALAD

Ingredients

- 2 (14.5 oz.) cans Italian-style diced tomatoes
- 1 (19 oz.) can cannellini beans, drained and rinsed
- 10 oz. fresh spinach, washed and chopped
- 8 oz. penne pasta
- 1/2 C. crumbled feta cheese

Directions

- Boil your pasta in water and salt for 9 mins then remove the liquids.
- At the same time get the following boiling: beans and tomatoes.
- Cook the mix for 13 mins with a low level of heat.
- Now combine in the spinach and cook everything for 4 more mins.
- Top the pasta with the sauce and cheese.
- Enjoy.

Amount per serving (4 total)

Timing Information:

Preparation	10 m
Cooking	15 m
Total Time	25 m

Nutritional Information:

Calories	460 kcal
Fat	5.9 g
Carbohydrates	79g
Protein	23.4 g
Cholesterol	17 mg
Sodium	593 mg

* Percent Daily Values are based on a 2,000 calorie diet.

EASY GREEK STYLE CHICKEN BREASTS

Ingredients

- 2 tbsps all-purpose flour, divided
- 1/2 tsp salt
- 1/4 tsp black pepper
- 1/4 lb. feta cheese, crumbled
- 1 tbsp fresh lemon juice
- 1 tsp dried oregano
- 6 boneless, skinless chicken breast halves, flatten to 1/2 thickness
- 2 tbsps olive oil
- 1 1/2 C. water
- 1 cube chicken bouillon, crumbled
- 2 C. loosely packed torn fresh spinach leaves
- 1 ripe tomato, chopped

Directions

- Get a bowl, mix: oregano, cheese, and lemon juice.
- Get a 2nd bowl, combine: bouillon, 1 C. of water, and flour.
- Dredge you chicken in a mix of pepper, salt, and flour.
- Then fold each piece and stake a toothpick through each one.

- Sear the chicken in oil for 3 mins per side. Then top the chicken with the contents of the 2nd bowl.
- Cook everything for 1 more min before adding tomatoes and spinach.
- Get everything boiling and then place a lid on the pot.
- Set the heat to low and let it all cook for 12 mins.
- Enjoy.

Amount per serving (6 total)

Timing Information:

Preparation	20 m
Cooking	20 m
Total Time	40 m

Nutritional Information:

Calories	239 kcal
Fat	10.2 g
Carbohydrates	4.8g
Protein	31 g
Cholesterol	85 mg
Sodium	686 mg

* Percent Daily Values are based on a 2,000 calorie diet.

BAKED GREEK POTATOES

Ingredients

- 1/3 C. olive oil
- 1 1/2 C. water
- 2 cloves garlic, finely chopped
- 1/4 C. fresh lemon juice
- 1 tsp dried thyme
- 1 tsp dried rosemary
- 2 cubes chicken bouillon
- ground black pepper to taste
- 6 potatoes, peeled and quartered

Directions

- Set your oven to 350 degrees before doing anything else.
- Get a bowl, combine: pepper, olive oil, bouillon, water, rosemary, water, thyme, garlic, and lemon juice.
- Layer the potatoes in a casserole dish and top everything with the lemon mix.
- Place some foil around the dish and cook the contents in the oven for 90 mins.
- Flip the potatoes every 30 mins while cooking.
- Enjoy.

Amount per serving (4 total)

Timing Information:

Preparation	20 m
Cooking	2 h
Total Time	2 h 20 m

Nutritional Information:

Calories	418 kcal
Fat	18.5 g
Carbohydrates	58.6g
Protein	7 g
Cholesterol	< 1 mg
Sodium	< 596 mg

* Percent Daily Values are based on a 2,000 calorie diet.

Artisan Orzo from Greece

Ingredients

- 1 1/2 C. uncooked orzo pasta
- 2 (6 oz.) cans marinated artichoke hearts, drained, liquid reserved
- 1 tomato, seeded and chopped
- 1 cucumber, seeded and chopped
- 1 red onion, chopped
- 1 C. crumbled feta cheese
- 1 (2 oz.) can black olives, drained
- 1/4 C. chopped fresh parsley
- 1 tbsp lemon juice
- 1/2 tsp dried oregano
- 1/2 tsp lemon pepper

Directions

- Boil your pasta in water and salt for 9 mins then remove all the liquids.
- Get a bowl, mix: lemon pepper, artichokes, oregano, lemon juice, tomatoes, pasta, parsley, cucumbers, olives, feta, and onions.

- Stir the contents, place a covering on the bowl, and put everything in the fridge for 2 hrs.
- Top the salad with the artichoke liquid and serve.
- Enjoy.

Amount per serving (6 total)

Timing Information:

Preparation	1 h 10 m
Cooking	10 m
Total Time	1 h 20 m

Nutritional Information:

Calories	348 kcal
Fat	10.2 g
Carbohydrates	53.2g
Protein	13.9 g
Cholesterol	22 mg
Sodium	615 mg

* Percent Daily Values are based on a 2,000 calorie diet.

GREEK BURGERS

Ingredients

- 1 lb. ground turkey
- 1 C. crumbled feta cheese
- 1/2 C. kalamata olives, pitted and sliced
- 2 tsps dried oregano
- ground black pepper to taste

Directions

- Get a bowl, combine: pepper, turkey, oregano, feta, and olives. Shape this into burgers and then grill each one for 6 mins.
- Flip the patty and cook it for 7 more mins.
- Enjoy.

Amount per serving (4 total)

Timing Information:

Preparation	10 m
Cooking	20 m
Total Time	40 m

Nutritional Information:

Calories	318 kcal
Fat	21.9 g
Carbohydrates	3.6g
Protein	25.5 g
Cholesterol	123 mg
Sodium	800 mg

* Percent Daily Values are based on a 2,000 calorie diet.

CHICKEN SOUP

Ingredients

- 8 C. chicken broth
- 1/2 C. fresh lemon juice
- 1/2 C. shredded carrots
- 1/2 C. chopped onion
- 1/2 C. chopped celery
- 6 tbsps chicken soup base
- 1/4 tsp ground white pepper
- 1/4 C. margarine
- 1/4 C. all-purpose flour
- 1 C. cooked white rice
- 1 C. diced, cooked chicken meat
- 16 slices lemon
- 8 egg yolks

Directions

- Get the following boiling: white pepper, chicken broth, soup base, celery, lemon juice, onions, and carrots.
- Set the heat to low and let the contents cook for 23 mins.

- Begin heating the flour and butter while stirring and then add in the soup while continuing to stir and cook the mix for 12 more mins.
- Now start whisking your eggs and then add in some soup while continuing to whisk.
- Add the entire mix to your soup and also add the chicken and the rice.
- When serving the soup top it with some pieces of lemon.
- Enjoy.

Amount per serving (16 total)

Timing Information:

Preparation	25 m
Cooking	40 m
Total Time	1 h 5 m

Nutritional Information:

Calories	124 kcal
Fat	6.6 g
Carbohydrates	9.1g
Protein	7.8 g
Cholesterol	110 mg
Sodium	1237 mg

* Percent Daily Values are based on a 2,000 calorie diet.

BEAN SALAD I

(CUCUMBERS, GARBANZOS, AND OLIVES)

Ingredients

- 2 (15 oz.) cans garbanzo beans, drained
- 2 cucumbers, halved lengthwise and sliced
- 12 cherry tomatoes, halved
- 1/2 red onion, chopped
- 2 cloves garlic, minced
- 1 (15 oz.) can black olives, drained and chopped
- 1 oz. crumbled feta cheese
- 1/2 C. Italian-style salad dressing
- 1/2 lemon, juiced
- 1/2 tsp garlic salt
- 1/2 tsp ground black pepper

Directions

- Get a bowl, toss: pepper, beans, garlic salt, cucumbers, lemon juice, tomatoes, dressing, onions, cheese, garlic, and olives.

- Place a covering on the bowl and put everything in the fridge for 3 hrs.
- Enjoy.

Amount per serving (8 total)

Timing Information:

Preparation	
Cooking	10 m
Total Time	2 h 10 m

Nutritional Information:

Calories	214 kcal
Fat	11.5 g
Carbohydrates	25.5g
Protein	5.2 g
Cholesterol	3 mg
Sodium	1067 mg

* Percent Daily Values are based on a 2,000 calorie diet.

Moussaka II

(Vegetarian Approved)

Ingredients

- 1 eggplant, thinly sliced
- 1 tbsp olive oil, or more as needed
- 1 large zucchini, thinly sliced
- 2 potatoes, thinly sliced
- 1 onion, sliced
- 1 clove garlic, chopped
- 1 tbsp white vinegar
- 1 (14.5 oz.) can whole peeled tomatoes, chopped
- 1/2 (14.5 oz.) can lentils, drained with liquid reserved
- 1 tsp dried oregano
- 2 tbsps chopped fresh parsley
- salt and ground black pepper to taste
- 1 C. crumbled feta cheese
- 1 1/2 tbsps butter
- 2 tbsps all-purpose flour
- 1 1/4 C. milk
- ground black pepper to taste
- 1 pinch ground nutmeg
- 1 egg, beaten
- 1/4 C. grated Parmesan cheese

Directions

- Get a bowl and add in your eggplants. Coat them with salt and let them sit for 40 mins.
- Now drain the resulting liquids and dry the eggplants with some paper towel.
- Set your oven to 375 degrees before doing anything else.
- Sear your zucchini and eggplants in oil for 4 mins per side. Then place the zucchini to the side on some paper towels.
- Now begin to stir fry your potatoes in the same pot for 6 mins then flip them and cook it all for 6 more mins. Place these to the side as well.
- Add in some more oil if needed and then start to stir fry your garlic and onions for 8 mins. Add the vinegar and get everything boiling.
- Once it is all boiling, set the heat to low, and cook the mix until everything is thick.
- Now add in: parsley, tomatoes, oregano, lentils, and half of the lentil juice.
- Place a lid on the pot and cook the contents for 17 mins with the same level of low heat.
- Get a casserole dish and add in 1/3 of the zucchini then the same amount of eggplant, then half of the following on top: feta, onions, and potatoes.
- Top everything with the tomato mix and then continue the layering.

- Once all of the ingredients have been used. Cooked the dish in the oven for 30 mins.
- Get the following boiling: milk, butter, and flour.
- Stir the contents as it begins to boil and once the mix is sauce like add in the nutmeg and pepper.
- Let the contents cool a bit then add in whisked eggs.
- Top the casserole with the egg mix and some parmesan and cook everything for 30 more mins.
- Enjoy.

Amount per serving (7 total)

Timing Information:

Preparation	30 m
Cooking	1 h 30 m
Total Time	2 h

Nutritional Information:

Calories	240 kcal
Fat	11.8 g
Carbohydrates	25.5g
Protein	10.2 g
Cholesterol	58 mg
Sodium	426 mg

* Percent Daily Values are based on a 2,000 calorie diet.

GREEK BURGERS II

Ingredients

- 1/2 lb. lean ground beef
- 1/2 lb. lean ground lamb
- 1/2 onion, grated
- 2 cloves garlic, pressed
- 1 slice bread, toasted and crumbled
- 1/2 tsp dried savory
- 1/2 tsp ground allspice
- 1/2 tsp ground coriander
- 1/2 tsp salt
- 1/2 tsp ground black pepper
- 1 dash ground cumin

Directions

- Get a bowl, mix: bread crumbs, cumin, savory, pepper, allspice, beef, onions, salt, coriander, and lamb.
- Mix the meats and spice with your hands until firm and then form the mix into 4 burgers.
- Grill these burgers for 8 mins per side.
- Enjoy.

Amount per serving (4 total)

Timing Information:

Preparation	10 m
Cooking	15 m
Total Time	25 m

Nutritional Information:

Calories	338 kcal
Fat	25.4 g
Carbohydrates	5.7g
Protein	20.3 g
Cholesterol	84 mg
Sodium	408 mg

* Percent Daily Values are based on a 2,000 calorie diet.

GREEK RICE

Ingredients

- 1/3 C. olive oil
- 2 onions, chopped
- 2 lbs fresh spinach, rinsed and stemmed
- 1 (8 oz.) can tomato sauce
- 2 C. water
- 1 tsp dried dill weed
- 1 tsp dried parsley
- salt and pepper to taste
- 1/2 C. uncooked white rice

Directions

- Stir fry your onions in olive oil until see-through then add in: spinach, water, and tomato sauce.
- Get everything boiling and then add: pepper, parsley, salt, and dill.
- Cook the mix for 2 mins while boiling then add the rice.
- Set the heat to low and cook everything for 27 mins.
- Enjoy.

Amount per serving (4 total)

Timing Information:

Preparation	5 m
Cooking	45 m
Total Time	50 m

Nutritional Information:

Calories	337 kcal
Fat	19.3 g
Carbohydrates	35.7g
Protein	9.8 g
Cholesterol	0 mg
Sodium	553 mg

* Percent Daily Values are based on a 2,000 calorie diet.

EASIEST GREEK CHICKEN

Ingredients

- 4 skinless, boneless chicken breast halves
- 1 C. extra virgin olive oil
- 1 lemon, juiced
- 2 tsps crushed garlic
- 1 tsp salt
- 1 1/2 tsps black pepper
- 1/3 tsp paprika

Directions

- Slice a few incisions into your pieces of chicken before doing anything else.
- Now get a bowl, combine: paprika, olive oil, pepper, lemon juice, salt, and garlic.
- Now add in the chicken and place the contents in the fridge for 8 hrs.
- Grill your chicken until fully done with indirect heat on the side of the grill with the grilling grates oiled.
- Enjoy.

Amount per serving (4 total)

Timing Information:

Preparation	10 m
Cooking	8 h
Total Time	8 h 30 m

Nutritional Information:

Calories	644 kcal
Fat	57.6 g
Carbohydrates	4g
Protein	27.8 g
Cholesterol	68 mg
Sodium	660 mg

* Percent Daily Values are based on a 2,000 calorie diet.

PARSLEY PASTA SALAD

Ingredients

- 2 (9 oz.) packages cheese tortellini
- 1/2 C. extra virgin olive oil
- 1/4 C. lemon juice
- 1/4 C. red wine vinegar
- 2 tbsps chopped fresh parsley
- 1 tsp dried oregano
- 1/2 tsp salt
- 6 eggs
- 1 lb. baby spinach leaves
- 1 C. crumbled feta cheese
- 1/2 C. slivered red onion

Directions

- Boil your pasta in water and salt for 9 mins then remove all the liquids.
- Get a bowl, mix: salt, olive oil, oregano, lemon juice, pasta, parsley, and vinegar.
- Stir the contents and then place everything in the fridge for 3 hrs.
- Get your eggs boiling in water, place a lid on the pot, and shut the heat.
- Let the eggs stand for 15 mins. Then peel, and cut them into quarters.

- Take out the bowl in the fridge and add in: onions, eggs, feta, and spinach.
- Stir everything before serving.
- Enjoy.

Amount per serving (8 total)

Timing Information:

Preparation	15 m
Cooking	15 m
Total Time	2 h 30 m

Nutritional Information:

Calories	486 kcal
Fat	30.3 g
Carbohydrates	35.7g
Protein	19.8 g
Cholesterol	196 mg
Sodium	836 mg

* Percent Daily Values are based on a 2,000 calorie diet.

ORZO SALAD II

Ingredients

- 1 C. uncooked orzo pasta
- 1/4 C. pitted green olives
- 1 C. diced feta cheese
- 3 tbsps chopped fresh parsley
- 3 tbsps chopped fresh dill
- 1 ripe tomato, chopped
- 1/4 C. virgin olive oil
- 1/8 C. lemon juice
- salt and pepper to taste

Directions

- Cook your orzo in boiling water with salt for 9 mins.
- Then remove the liquid and run the pasta under cool water.
- Now get a bowl, combine: tomato, olive, dill, feta, parsley, and orzo.
- Get a 2nd bowl, mix: lemon juice pepper, salt, and oil.
- Combine both bowls and toss everything.
- Place the mix in the fridge until cold.
- Enjoy.

Amount per serving (6 total)

Timing Information:

Preparation	15 m
Cooking	10 m
Total Time	25 m

Nutritional Information:

Calories	329 kcal
Fat	19.6 g
Carbohydrates	28.1g
Protein	10.9 g
Cholesterol	37 mg
Sodium	614 mg

* Percent Daily Values are based on a 2,000 calorie diet.

GREEK FALAFEL

Ingredients

- 1 (19 oz.) can garbanzo beans, rinsed and drained
- 1 small onion, finely chopped
- 2 cloves garlic, minced
- 1 1/2 tbsps chopped fresh cilantro
- 1 tsp dried parsley
- 2 tsps ground cumin
- 1/8 tsp ground turmeric
- 1/2 tsp baking powder
- 1 C. fine dry bread crumbs
- 3/4 tsp salt
- 1/4 tsp cracked black peppercorns
- 1 quart vegetable oil for frying

Directions

- Get a bowl, combine: pepper, onions, salt, garlic, bread crumbs, cilantro, baking powder, parsley, mashed garbanzos, turmeric, and cumin.
- Form the contents into small balls and make about 20 of them.
- Deep fry these falafels in hot oil until golden.
- Enjoy.

Amount per serving (6 total)

Timing Information:

Preparation	25 m
Cooking	7 m
Total Time	32 m

Nutritional Information:

Calories	317 kcal
Fat	16.8 g
Carbohydrates	35.2g
Protein	7.2 g
Cholesterol	0 mg
Sodium	724 mg

* Percent Daily Values are based on a 2,000 calorie diet.

THANKS FOR READING! JOIN THE CLUB AND KEEP ON COOKING WITH 6 MORE COOKBOOKS....

http://bit.ly/1TdrStv

 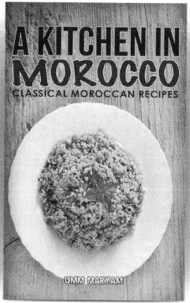 

To grab the box sets simply follow the link mentioned above, or tap one of book covers.

This will take you to a page where you can simply enter your email address and a PDF version of the box sets will be emailed to you.

Hope you are ready for some serious cooking!

http://bit.ly/1TdrStv

COME ON...
LET'S BE FRIENDS :)

We adore our readers and love connecting with them socially.

Like BookSumo on Facebook and let's get social!

Facebook

And also check out the BookSumo Cooking Blog.

Food Lover Blog

Made in the USA
Lexington, KY
23 May 2018